A SWING OF THE PENDULUM
CANON LAW IN MODERN SOCIETY
Monsignor W. Onclin Chair 1996

KATHOLIEKE UNIVERSITEIT LEUVEN
Faculteit Kerkelijk Recht
Faculty of Canon Law

A SWING OF THE PENDULUM

CANON LAW
IN MODERN SOCIETY

Monsignor W. Onclin Chair 1996

UITGEVERIJ PEETERS
LEUVEN
1996

C.I.P. Koninklijke Bibliotheek Albert I

ISBN 90-6831-803-9
D.1996/0602/28

© 1996 Uitgeverij Peeters, Bondgenotenlaan 153, B-3000 Leuven (Belgium)

INHOUDSTAFEL / TABLE OF CONTENTS

UNE MESSE EST POSSIBLE.
OVER DE NABIJHEID VAN KERK EN GELOOF

"Une messe est possible". Dat schreef de voormalige Franse president François Mitterrand toen hij op 6 januari 1996, twee dagen voor zijn dood, en zich volledig bewust van het naderende einde, zijn laatste wil verwoordde. Drie witte vellen papier, half formaat, handgeschreven met blauwe inkt. Mitterrand meldde dat hij na zijn dood geen toespraken wilde, geen bloemen, geen kransen, behalve twee boeketjes, een tuiltje theerozen en een tuiltje irissen, paars en geel. Maar hij schreef dus ook: *"Une messe est possible"*.

Een mens schrijft zoveel, zeker als hij maar weinig tijd meer heeft. En Mitterrand was geen heilige, ofschoon wel een uiterst boeiend man. Maar er gaat hoe dan ook iets fascinerends uit van die laatste mededeling. Er zit aangrijpende terughoudendheid in. Een schoorvoetende niet-afwijzing. Vaal is het licht dat op deze scène valt. Maar een mis, die mogelijk is, en niet meer, en die er dus wel komt, zij *is* er gekomen, zoiets laat niet onberoerd … De schoonheid van de niet-afwijzing, zij gaat precies wegens haar aarzelende aanwezigheid recht naar het hart.

Het wat bizarre levenseinde van François Mitterrand — hij stierf uiteindelijk zonder zijn familie in de ochtend van 8 januari, achter de gesloten witte gordijnen van zijn Parijse woning — kan tot allerlei beschouwingen aanleiding geven, wat op zich al een mooie gedachte is. Het wijst in elk geval óók op de zoektocht van iemand die zich beklaagde over de geestelijke droogte van deze tijd en die voor zichzelf geen andere keuze zag dan zich spiritueel te verdiepen in het geheim van leven en dood. En zo stond hij niet eindeloos ver van een instituut waarvan hij zich ook wel verwijderd had. *Une messe est possible.* Opeens komt de kerk weer wat dichterbij, helpt ze even een wat onwezenlijke eenheid tussen de Franse bevolking smeden, hoewel dit alles natuurlijk ook weer niet betekent dat de Franse of Westerse samenleving meteen weer een stukje katholieker aan het worden is.

Maar toch schuilt in het verhaal van François Mitterrand en zijn mis die mogelijk is, een soort van verrassende en plotse nabijheid van Kerk en geloof, zij het met enige nauwelijks formuleerbare gêne, zij het misschien omdat andere symbolen ongeloofwaardiger, nog ongeloofwaardiger lijken op momenten waarop vluchten niet meer kan. Die nabijheid zou ik eigenlijk ook het kerkelijk recht willen toewensen, want om dit mooie vak is het ons vandaag te doen. En ja, kerkelijk recht blijft al met al een wat barse en een wat dwarse discipline. Het beschrijft de hardere, schijnbaar minder buigzame, wat grimmiger structurele facetten van een instituut Kerk dat zelf al, bij heel wat van onze tijdgenoten, een gevoel van vervreemding opwekt. Om vandaag de dag canoniek recht bespreekbaar te maken moeten, gezwind of moeizaam, twee hindernissen worden genomen.

Eerst moet hij die ons vak wil verdedigen, afrekenen met het vooroordeel dat er alleen buiten de Kerk heil is, dat deze Kerk niet deugt want niet authentiek is, dat zij niet méér is dan een gepasseerd station in de grote zoektocht van de mens, dat het intellectueel superieur is niet of niet meer kerkelijk te zijn. Ga daar maar eens tegenaan, in deze tijd, waarin niet zelden ook waardevolle signalen worden uitgezonden die bevestigen dat deze stelling gewoon waar is.

Maar neem nu dat het toch lukt sympathie voor de Kerk te winnen, dat de ontsporing niet tot regel wordt uitgeroepen en het kind niet verdwijnt met het badwater, dan nog blijft de vraag rondom het bestaansrecht en de werking van het kerkelijk recht. Doodt het niet alle mysterie? Verstikt het niet elke vorm van engagement? Schept het geen hardheid waar liefde moet heersen? Vervreemdt het niet daar waar nabijheid moet zijn? En de vraag wordt niet per se in concreto gesteld. Nee, het lijkt vaak allemaal aan het recht zelf te liggen, dat te bot oogt, te hoekig, te wanstaltig om met breekbare begrippen als liefde en geloof op weg te kunnen gaan.

Het is natuurlijk duidelijk dat recht, wanneer het repressief en levensver is, of op die manier wordt toegepast, enthousiasme fnuikt, initiatieven keldert en, vooral, diep in het hart diep ongelukkig maakt. Maar evenmin als de Kerk niet per se heilloos is, voert recht niet altijd tot verwijdering en vervreemding. Goed recht doet dat niet. Tja … Natuurlijk doorziet u de truc die ik bij deze redenering hanteer. Het mogelijk schadelijke karakter van het kerkelijk recht wordt weggeabstraheerd, zo in de stijl van: kerkelijk recht is niet schadelijk, want het hoeft niet schadelijk te zijn. Te gemakkelijk natuurlijk. De vraag moet luiden: is het *nu bestaande* kerkelijk recht schadelijk?

Het is soms een *beetje* schadelijk. Het is menselijk. Het blijft soms wat te ver van de mensen af en schiet om die reden tekort. Zo heeft het, naar mijn aanvoelen, niet zo heel veel echt heel moois in petto voor mensen die dingen schrijven zoals *"une messe est possible"*. Ze krijgen hun mis, dat is per slot van rekening wel aardig, maar zij hebben in het canoniek recht niet echt een helder juridisch statuut. De ondernemers van bochtige zoektochten, de liefhebbers van mogelijke missen, zij missen het heldere statuut dat onder meer de *haereticus* toevalt, de ketter, hij die, zoals canon 751 omschrijft, na het ontvangen van het doopsel, een of andere waarheid die met goddelijk of katholiek geloof moet worden geloofd, hardnekkig ontkent of in twijfel trekt. De ketter loopt volgens canon 1364 § 1 een excommunicatie van rechtswege op en kan ook elders in de Codex op de aandacht van de wetgever rekenen. En wie verlangt niet naar een beetje aandacht?

Impliciet gaat ook het huidige wetboek uit van een geloof dat er bij het doopsel wel zal zijn en dat nadien dreigt af te brokkelen, waardoor iemand dan mogelijk ketter wordt, of misschien alleen maar schismaticus of zelfs wel apostaat. In die zin strijdt de Codex tegen erosie en verlies, probeert hij een neerwaartse spiraal tegen te gaan, soms toch, niet zelden.

En er ontbreekt tegelijk een rechtsstatuut voor een heel courant in onze hedendaagse maatschappij opduikend type mens. Iemand die wordt gedoopt, maar al van bij het begin niet heel hard gelooft, evenmin als zijn ouders trouwens, en die dan, daarna, misschien wat argeloos, achteloos, wie weet ook soms hardnekkig, zoekt naar wat verborgen is, naar diepgang, naar de geheimen van leven en dood. En die dan, misschien, terwijl hij ook nog even aan rozen of tulpen of fresia's denkt, heel kort laat weten … *une messe est possible*. Wie deze moeizame, soms opwaartse, soms zijwaartse, soms helaas wat neerwaartse weg volgt, wordt in de Codex schijnbaar minder liefgehad, het wetboek noemt hem alleszins niet bij een naam.

Maar een wetboek kan niet volmaakt zijn. De canonist die er gedeelten van bekritiseert, is het zelf wellicht nog een heel stuk minder. Een beetje vervreemding behoeft niet uit te lopen in verwijdering. Het vigerende canoniek recht is geen doodlopend spoor, geen somber symbool van een voorbije tijd. Met de huidige Codex *kan* zeker creatief worden gewerkt. Zoals paus Johannes-Paulus II schrijft in de apostolische constitutie *Sacrae disciplinae leges* ademt het wetboek de geest van het meest recente concilie. Het biedt bovendien, precies omdat het rechtsregels bevat, die *dus* praktische toepassing behoeven, ruimte voor interpretatie, zoals onder meer canon 17 die beschrijft.

Op die wijze, langs de edele kunst der interpretatie, wordt het recht vaak levendiger en komt het naderbij. Bovendien is er, naast de rechtsregels zelf, de rechtspraak, waarvan monseigneur J.M. Serrano Ruiz een eminent beoefenaar is. De jurisprudentie is, in elk gezond rechtssysteem, strikt noodzakelijk om verstarring te vermijden. Zij zorgt ervoor dat de rechtsregel niet verschraalt tot een skelet. Zij houdt het recht alert en aantrekkelijk. Jong ook, al is de regel oud. De jurisprudentie schrijft een verhaal. Op haar kan *mutatis mutandis* worden toegepast wat de Franse romancier Jean d'Ormesson in zijn laatste boek *Presque rien sur presque tout* schreef, in alle eenvoud: *"Ce qu'il y a de mieux dans la pensée, c'est sa souplesse."* We moeten ons hier hoeden voor goedkope effecten. Natuurlijk mag die soepelheid niet tot normloosheid leiden, maar het tegendeel is evenzeer waar: de norm mag niet voeren tot de afwezigheid van elke beweging. Lieve buigzaamheid voorkomt niet zelden barsten.

Omdat wij geloven dat kerkelijk recht levensnabij en aantrekkelijk kan zijn, organiseert de faculteit kerkelijk recht van de K.U.Leuven, die door onze academische overheid lyrisch *bijzondere* faculteit wordt genoemd, jaarlijks de *Monsignor W. Onclin Chair for Comparative Canon Law*. Telkens weer worden bij deze gelegenheid twee canonisten van wereldfaam uitgenodigd. Vorig jaar waren dat professor R.G.W. Huysmans en monseigneur C. Burke, vandaag spreken monseigneur J.M. Serrano Ruiz en professor F.G. Morrisey. Al deze experten genieten bekendheid wegens hun uitmuntende wetenschappelijke prestaties, maar ook wegens het aanstekelijke enthousiasme waarmee ze hun vak beoefenen.

Zo slagen de twee sprekers van vandaag erin van canoniek recht een wetenschap te maken die niet alleen tot de verbeelding spreekt, maar dat bovendien doet in positieve zin.

Monseigneur J.M. Serrano Ruiz, auditeur aan de Romeinse Rota, behoorde tot de eerste rechters die de personalistische huwelijksvisie van Vaticanum II ook kerkrechtelijk gestalte hebben gegeven, lang voordat de nieuwe Codex werd uitgevaardigd.

Professor F.G. Morrisey, hoogleraar aan St Paul University in Ottawa, zonder twijfel een van de bekendste canonisten van Amerika en, onder meer, een wereldvermaard expert op het vlak van katholieke gezondheidsinstellingen, is de tweede spreker. Hij heeft zowel gevoel voor realiteit als voor diepere dromen en verwachtingen, wat ook hem tot een uitermate mens- en levensnabij canonist maakt.

En die laatste eigenschappen blijven van cruciaal belang, wat ook het antwoord weze op de in canonieke kringen onvermijdelijke vraag of ons vak nu een juridische of een theologische discipline is, en, zo het een theologische discipline zou blijken te zijn, of het dan een juridische dan wel een theologische methode dient te omarmen. En zo verder, of wat dacht u?

François Mitterrand, zijn drie velletjes papier, de blauwe inkt, *une messe est possible* … Zij vormden een te mooi en vooral een te dwingend excuus om al deze vragen niet nog een keer te moeten behandelen …

Prof. dr. Rik Torfs
Voorzitter faculteit kerkelijk recht.

UNE MESSE EST POSSIBLE.
A CHALLENGE FOR CANON LAW

"Une messe est possible", wrote the former French president François Mitterrand when he articulated on January 6 1996, two days before his death and fully aware of his coming end, his last will and testament. Three white sheets, small size, hand-written with blue ink. Mitterrand declared that after his death, he wanted no speeches, no flowers, no wreaths but only two little bouquets, one made out of tea roses and the other of irises, purple and yellow. But he also wrote: *"Une messe est possible"*.

One can write so much, especially when the sands of time are running out. Mitterrand was no saint, although he was an extremely captivating person. But there is something fascinating about his last announcement. It breathes out a moving reticence. A reluctant non-refusal. Pale is the light that falls upon this scene. But a mass, that is just possible and nothing more, which will be celebrated, and was celebrated, touches the world. The beauty of the non-refusal goes because of its wavering presence directly to the heart.

The somewhat bizarre end of life of François Mitterrand — he died eventually without his family, in the morning of January 8, behind the white closed curtains of his house in Paris — could bring about all kinds of considerations, in itself already a beautiful thought. It also points out the quest of someone who lamented the spiritual waste land of our times and who saw for himself no other choice than to bury himself in the secret of life and death. And in this way, he finally stood less apart from the institute he parted from. *Une messe est possible.* And suddenly the church approaches a little bit more, and it helps for an instant to weld the somewhat illusory unity between the French population, although of course it does not mean that the French and Western society are becoming more catholic again.

And yet, the story of François Mitterrand and his mass that is possible, contains a certain unexpected and sudden nearness of church and faith, although with some kind of embarrassment that one can hardly express, and maybe because other symbols are just more or much more unbelievable in these moments where there is no running away. That nearness I would also like to grant Canon Law, the real topic of today's session. Indeed, Canon Law remains a fairly stern and firm discipline. It describes the hard, apparently less lenient and rather grim structural aspects of the institute Church, that rouses a lot of our contemporaries already to a sentiment of alienation. In order to make Canon Law in today's society debatable, one has to overcome two hindrances, smoothly or arduously.

He who wants to defend our profession, has to deal in the first place with the prejudice that there in only bliss outside the church, since the church is no good, not authentic, nothing more than a passed stop in the great quest for the truth, that it is intellectually superior to be non-churchgoing. Try to defeat this, in our modern times where not seldom other meaningful signals are sent, confirming that this approach is simply true.

But even if we could gain more sympathy for the Church, and if the lapse were not declared as rule, the question concerning the right to exist and the functioning of Canon Law, still remains. Does it not kill all mystery? Does it not smother every form of commitment? Does it not create harshness where love should rule? Does it not alienate there where it should bind? The question is not even raised in concreto. No, the law seems to be to blame for itself, because it appears too blunt, too angular, too distorted to handle fragile notions like love and faith.

It is of course true that law, when it is repressive and far away from life, or used in that manner, cripples all enthusiasm, breaks down all initiatives and above all, makes one deep down in the heart deeply unhappy. But just as the Church is not entirely without bliss, law does not always lead to elimination and alienation. Good law does not do this. Well, of course you can all see through the tricks I use in this argumentation. The possible harmful character of Canon Law has been drawn away, a bit like the comment: Canon Law is not harmful, because it need not be harmful. Too easy of course. The question should be: is the now existing Canon Law harmful?

It is sometimes a little bit harmful. It is human. It remains sometimes too far away from humans and that is why it fails. It does not have, in my opinion, an awful lot in store for people who write things like *"Une messe est possible"*. They will receive their mass, which has to be acknowledged, but they do not have a very clear juridical statute in the Code of Canon Law. Those who endeavour troublesome investigations, those who adore possible masses, must miss the clear statute that is given to for instance the *haereticus*, the heretic, he who, according to canon 751, holds an obstinate post-baptismal denial of some truth that must be believed with divine and catholic faith, or an obstinate doubt concerning the same. The heretic incurs automatic excommunication according to canon 1364 § 1 and can also elsewhere in the Code of Canon Law count on the attention of the legislator. And don't we all want some attention?

Implicitly, the current Code of Canon Law assumes that faith is present at the time of baptism and that it risks to wilt later on, turning the person possibly into an heretic, or maybe only a schismatic or even an apostate. In this way, the Code fights against the erosion and loss, and tries to stop the downward spiral movement, sometimes, not seldom.

There is also another legal statute missing for the kind of person we find so often and regularly in our modern society. Someone who was baptised, but did never really believe that strongly, nor did his parents by the way, and who then maybe a bit thoughtlessly and carelessly and maybe also stubbornly, seeks for what is hidden, for depth and the secrets of life and death. And who, maybe while also just thinking about roses, tulips or freesias, announces briefly ... *une messe est possible*. He who follows this somewhat tiresome, sometimes upward, sometimes sideward, but unfortunately also sometimes downward course, is apparently loved less in the Code of Canon Law, he is in any case not mentioned by his name.

But a Code cannot be perfect. The canonist who criticises parts of it, is probably even a whole lot less perfect. A little bit of alienation need not turn out into elimination. The prevailing canon law is no dead end trail, no gloomy symbol of times gone by. One can definitely work creatively with the current Code. Like Pope John-Paul II wrote in the apostolic constitution *Sacrae disciplinae leges*, the Code breathes the spirit of the most recent Council. It offers furthermore, exactly because it contains rules of law, that thus need a practical application, room for interpretation, just like canon 17 for instance, describes it.

In this way, along the noble art of interpretation, law becomes often more vivid and intimate. Next to the rules of law in itself, there is also the jurisprudence, of which Monsignor J.M. Serrano Ruiz is an eminent practitioner. The jurisprudence is in every healthy legal system strictly necessary in order to avoid rigidity. It protects the legal rule from turning into a skeleton. It makes law alert and attractive and young, although the rules are old. The jurisprudence tells a story. One can apply here mutatis mutandis the words the French novelist Jean d'Ormesson wrote in his last novel *Presque rien sur presque tout*: *"Ce qu'il y a de mieux dans la pensée, c'est sa souplesse."* We must beware here of cheap effects. Of course, souplesse should not lead to a standardless situation, but the opposite is neither true: the standard may not lead to the absence of movement. Kind flexibility prevents not seldom bursting.

Because we believe that Canon Law can be attractive and close by, the Faculty of Canon Law of the K. U. Leuven, lyrically termed by the academic authorities *special faculty*, organises yearly the Monsignor W. Onclin Chair for Comparative Canon Law. Each time two canonists of world wide fame are invited for the occasion. Last year Professor R.G.W. Huysmans and Monsignor C. Burke came and this year Monsignor J.M. Serrano Ruiz and Professor F.G. Morrisey will speak to you. All these experts are widely known because of their outstanding scientific achievements, but also because of their contagious enthusiasm they put into their profession.

In this manner, the two lecturers of today succeed in turning Canon Law into a science that does not only appeal to the imagination, but above all do so in a positive sense.

Monsignor J.M. Serrano Ruiz, auditor of the Roman Rota, is one of the first judges who gave the personalistic vision on marriage of Vatican II also a canon law frame, long before the new Code was enacted.

Professor F.G. Morrisey, professor at Saint Paul University in Ottawa, and without doubt one of the most famous canonists of America and among other things a world-wide expert on the catholic healthcare institutions, is the second speaker. He has a strong feeling for both reality and the deeper dreams and expectations, that make him into a extreme human and approachable canonist.

These last qualifications remain of crucial importance, whatever the answer to the in our circles inevitable question is: whether our profession is a juridical or a theological discipline, and whether when it is a theological discipline, it embraces a juridical or a theological method. And so on, or what did you think?

François Mitterrand, his three sheets of paper, the blue ink, *une messe est possible* … They made an excuse too beautiful and compelling to ask and treat all these questions once more.

Prof. dr. Rik Torfs
Dean Faculty of Canon Law.

Translation by Ruth Nys.

ACERCA DEL CARÁCTER PERSONAL
DEL MATRIMONIO:
DIGRESIONES Y RETORNOS

Quisiera dejar sentado desde el principio muy claramente que no vamos a tratar en concreto de algunos puntos determinados de la dogmática y Jurisprudencia canónica matrimonial — aunque será imprescindible ocuparnos de ellos —: sino sobre una suerte de planteamiento o presupuesto común a todos ellos. Por lo que la utilidad de estas lecciones no será escasa, sino mayor que la que hubiera podido derivarse de una atención específica a un punto concreto. Tengo también presente de que se trata de un trabajo universitario o doctrinal: distinto por tanto del que habría de realizarse en una Sentencia o pronunciamiento judicial sobre un caso determinado. De ahí que nos sea permitida una mayor amplitud de miras sobre aspectos que aunque a primera vista pudieran parecer abstractos, son sin embargo presupuestos necesarios para una mayor y mejor análisis existencial de los casos que se presenten. Se va a dar una especie de paradoja en estas palabras. Como hemos dicho, pretenden ser principios generales, verdades fundamentalísimas; de otra parte quisieran ir cargadas de existencialidad, de fidelidad a la vida real a costa de alejarse de la abstracción. Así será en efecto: una especulación al servício de los datos reales.

Quisiera poner en guardia en fin frente a otra posible malentendido. Pues cuando se afrontan puntos fundamentales en seguida se presume una actitud radical de enfrentamiento con los vigentes. Parece que es lícito divergir en la interpretación; hay que ser intransigentes en los principios y rechazar en seguida como heteredoxo al que parte de otros diversos. Pienso que no ha de ser necesariamente así y que nada hay más lejos de nuestra intención. Pienso que estas ideas, si bien no dudo que renovadoras de nuestros habituales puntos de vista, se integran sin dificultad en ellos y suponen más bien un complemento que un contraste. Iluminar aspectos hasta ahora no demasiado explorados de la realidad no significa demoler los anteriores sino enriquecerlos con una visión totalizante. No se trata pues de ser revolucionarios: sí de llamar la atención sobre notas del pacto conyugal que serán útiles no sólo en la consideración jurídico-canónica de él, sino también en su vertiente dogmática, moral, pastoral etc.[1] Como cuestión de hecho se han de tocar puntos fundamentales que habrán de repercutir en la visión canónica del matrimonio y de las Causas de Nulidad matrimonial en cuanto éstas atañen al ser o no ser mismo del matrimonio. Es éste un esfuerzo por llegar al núcleo común y esencial del matrimonio canónico y evitar metodológicamente ese excesivo análisis a que sometemos el misterio cristiano, solicitados por la minuciosidad de unas normas que enuncian o suponen a la vez la vigencia del derecho natural y la necesidad de proteger la seguridad del vínculo[2]. Es cierto que con el análisis, minucioso por demás, parecemos alcanzar ventajas didácticas y normativas; pero también corremos el riesgo de no advertir lo fundamental por eso mismo que primero y menos expresable de forma inmediata y precisa.

Por no poner sino un ejemplo sobre el que luego volveremos: ¿quién se ha entretenido hasta ahora en ahondar en la naturaleza *dual* del matrimonio en su aspecto sacramental? ¿quién ha echado de ver con la trascendencia que tal afirmación supone que en la economía de la salvación todos los sacramentos son unipersonales y solo el matrimonio supone dos personas existe y consiste en ambas y no se da sino en la comunión y el consentimiento?[3] Y así otros aspectos.

Permitámonos pues algunas digresiones del trillado camino en que normalmente se desenvuelven nuestros coloquios canónicos y conversaciones 'profesionales' e intentemos un salto a las altas cumbres en las que ese río caudaloso y no siempre apacible que es el estudio canónico del matrimonio encuentra su manantial. Pero no olvidemos nunca que hemos de volver a casa, a ese hogar seguro e inconmovible que es el instituto matrimonial, por el que tan diligentemente vela la Iglesia.

Ante todo interesa fijar la nota de *unicidad* que conviene al matrimonio. No sólo porque viene a ser el tema casi único de que se ocupan

---

[1] Evidentemente el carácter personal del matrimonio no le conviene sólo y ni siquiera radicalmente en su formalidad jurídica sino en cuanto matrimonio *ut sic*. En cualquier caso en ese *ser* del matrimonio que se encuentra en todos sus aspectos: cf. SERRANO RUIZ, J.M., "Él carácter personal del matrimonio: presupuestos y perspectivas para las Causas canónicas de nulidad" en *Iustus Iudex*, Festgabe für Paul Wesemann, ed. Ludgerus-Verlag, Essen, 1990, 310-329.

[2] La observación es especialmente aplicable a los cc. 1095 ss.: que aunque versan sobre aspectos fundamentales del acto humano (personal) se extienden en múltiples detalles.

[3] Cf. una Sentencia c. SERRANO, de 13 diciembre 1991 en *SRR Dec. seu Sent.* 83 (1991), 756-787.

nuestros tribunales, sino también porque su identidad jurídica se aparta de cualquier otra[4]. Y ello tanto es así que no tengo inconveniente en reconocer que nuestras *digresiones* no serán *del* matrimonio, sino *en el* matrimonio: es decir no nos apartarán del matrimonio sino que nos introducirán en lo más recóndito de él, en su corazón: y nunca mejor empleada esta metáfora que aplicada al misterio cristiano del amor. Como en tantas otras ocasiones lo más profundo resulta ser lo más inexplorado, si bien la lógica hubiera exigido comenzar por ahí. En cualquier modo no hemos de sentirnos ni solos ni humillados por ello en nuestra condición de obreros del matrimonio. No sino mucho después de estar familiarizado con el Evangelio, caí en la cuenta en la gran paradoja que encierra el comienzo de la parábola del Buen Samaritano: el doctor de la Ley que se acerca a Jesús y le pregunta por el camino de la salvación. Y el Maestro que responde con método mayéutico intentando comprometer al demandante en la pregunta: *¿Qué lees, que hay escrito en la Ley?* — Y el maestro que responda con la letra. Y el Profeta que le acucia. Y el curioso que tiene que encontrar una salida: *¿Quién es mi prójimo?* — Para mí que la introducción pudo ser más larga: ¿cómo tú eres maestro de la Ley y no eres capaz de reconocer la segunda palabra de ella? — Así también nosotros seríamos puestos en un compromiso serio si nos preguntaran por el núcleo fundamental del matrimonio. Un preclaro miembro de vuestra comunidad nacional dijo en su obra fundamental que *el extraño destino de las realidades más importantes del hombre es que sólo son accesibles a la vivencia y no a la descripción racional*[5]. No disponemos nosotros — y seguramente nadie — de una vivencia de la realidad fundamental del matrimonio; ni tampoco podemos pretender expresarla en cualquier fórmula lógica que le sea adecuada. Pero no hemos de dejar de reconocer con todo que es importante intentarlo y llegar hasta donde se pueda[6].

Hechas estas observaciones preliminares, vengamos ya a nuestro título: *"Reflexiones acerca del carácter personal del matrimonio"*. En torno a él he experimentado alguna duda ya en cuanto a los términos utilizados. *"Carácter"*: Alguien hubiera preferido índole; pero el vocablo

---

[4] Cf. SERRANO RUIZ, J.M., "Acerca de algunas notas específicas del derecho y deber conyugal", en *Revista Española de Derecho Canónico*, 85 (1974), 5 ss.

[5] Cf. MOELLER, Ch., *Literatura del siglo XX y Christianismo*, ed. cast., Madrid, 1955, tom. II, 360.

[6] Cabría la analogía con cuanto dice el Concilio Vaticano I sobre la inteligencia no exhaustiva pero sí fructuosísima de los misterios de la Fe (cf. DENZINGER, *Enchiridion Symbolorum*, n. 1796).

se me antojaba demasiado latino y genérico; más propio tal vez para cualificar a las *personas* que a lo *personal* — ¿*Naturaleza* personal? De ningún modo; sólo sería aceptable en la acepción metafísica de la palabra como sinónimo de esencia; pero aún así sugeriría de alguna manera la idea que se quiere alejar: la presencia de ninguna realidad objetiva, por lo demás como física, en el núcleo esencial del matrimonio, distinta de las personas mismas de los esposos. ¿Por qué no, entonces, *esencia personal* del matrimonio? Las dificultades llegan ahora desde el otro extremo. Demasiada abstracción; casi hasta la contradicción con el concepto mismo de persona y personalidad embebido del todo de existencialidad. ¿*Visión personal*, entonces? Cierto que no; llevaría a pensar en posturas de ensayo y parecer subjetivos. Y si bien la nuestra lo sea en principio, como hemos ya advertido tiene la pretensión de llegar hasta el núcleo mismo del problema.

Carácter por tanto. Con todo el peso de las resonancias clásicas, históricas, gramaticales, hasta culturales, antropológicas y sicológicas que encierra la palabra. Pero *carácter* que muestra a la vez lo que más profundamente *incide* en el modo de ser de una realidad y al mismo tiempo la distingue de cualquier otra y la identifica de un modo inequívoco. Y cuando tal núcleo esencial e identificante es un todo complejo y no fácilmente determinable hay que tener en cuenta todas las componentes para llegar a una idea lo más exacta posible del *carácter*, de la formalidad de que se trata, que exalta y distingue.

Así lo *personal*. La importancia de la *persona* y de lo *personal* no es ciertamente una conquista o un progreso en la renovada visión del matrimonio. Es antes que nada un *signo de los tiempos* que se manifiesta en todo: en el derecho público y privado, constitucional, de orden interno e internacional, en la Iglesia — en las Iglesias — y en la sociedad civil. Es más una inspiración común y total que una norma o conjunto de normas en torno a un instituto jurídico concreto. Ella como es lógico se hace más acuciante en aquellos espacios de la sicología, de la moral, de la sociología o del derecho en el cual el ser humano ocupa una posición de mayor protagonismo inmediato. Sería inexacto afirmar que es sólo en el matrimonio donde la Iglesia ha encontrado la oportunidad de acoger y desarrollar este movimiento, cuando toda la espléndida Constitución Pastoral *Gaudium et Spes* del Concilio Vaticano II, por no hablar de otros documentos conciliares, está penetrada de tal inspiración y punto de partida. El matrimonio es una aplicación, por lo demás oportunísima, de cuanto venimos diciendo acerca del Derecho que se ocupa más inmediatamente del hombre y de su mundo.

Cierto que no podemos entrar aquí y ahora en toda la especulación intelectual reciente y en toda la literatura que se ocupa de la *persona* y de lo *personal*[7]. Pero también me interesa señalar — siguiendo en la glosa de nuestro título — que he dicho carácter *personal* y no *personalista*. La expresión *personalista* — o peor todavía *personalistico/a* — se lee con frecuencia a propósito del matrimonio en dos contextos: o con relación a la ya lejana controversia entre finalidades *personalisticas* y finalidades *institucionalisticas* que tuvo en H. DOMS su más conocido y censurado representante[8]; o por contraposición con una llamada concepción *institucionalística* — que también en este caso podría mejor, pienso, llamarse *institucional* — del matrimonio mismo[9]. Pero nuestro uso de la expresión *personal* — carácter *personal*: y no *personalista* o *personalístico* — pretende llamar la atención sobre aspectos integrativos y no disociativos entre *persona* e *instituto*, por ejemplo; o entre *humano y personal*. Realidades que se dan a la vez y en las que no se trata de negar una para afirmar con más fuerza la otra; sino de profundizar juntos ambos aspectos para enriquecerlos y asegurarlos mutuamente, pues juntos se encuentran en al matrimonio cristiano. No debilitaremos lo personal hasta reducirlo a un individualismo indiferenciado; ni exaltaremos lo institucional hasta hacerlo insensible a las exigencias de lo personal: sino que reconoceremos en todos los seres humanos las irrenunciables prerrogativas de la '*personeidad*' — de acuerdo con la feliz expresión de mi filósofo connacional X. ZUBIRI[10] — y en el instituto sus nobilísimos orígines y sus altísimas finalidades que lo hacen connatural y consustancial a la persona humana.

En nuestras por fuerza limitadas, que no intrascendentes ni tediosas, digresiones sobre los principios, lógicos y culturales del matrimonio

[7] Cf. "El carácter personal del matrimonio", cit., en *Iustus Iudex*, p. 311, n. 2.

[8] Cf. *Vom Sinn und Zweck der Ehe. Eine systematische Studie*, Breslau, 1935; *AAS* 36 (1944), 103.

[9] Se ha dado a veces el intento, muy loable, de recurrir a la voz y a la idea de *instituto jurídico* para evitar la a todas luces desafortunada expresión de *contrato* aplicada al matrimonio. Precisamente por la amplitud que tiene el concepto de *instituto* tal intento puede resultar frustrado. ¿Acaso el contrato no es un instituto? — Como hemos visto, lo importante es explicar el matrimonio desde el matrimonio mismo y no desde otras figuras por más que referibles a una cierta semejanza a él.

[10] Cf. ZUBIRI, X., *Sobre la esencia*, Madrid, 1962, 504-505.

vamos a visitar la Palabra de Dios, la Antropología y el Derecho a propósito de la *personeidad* del matrimonio.

Es difícil caminar de prisa a través de la Revelación. Y más aún cuanto que el matrimonio es uno de los temas que atraviesa todo el mensaje de Dios a la humanidad desde los orígenes de la creación hasta las Bodas reales de la Esposa con el Cordero.

Pero puede servir de frase emblemática una interpretación concreta de las palabras del comienzo: *"Por ello dejará el hombre a su padre y a su madre y se unirá a su mujer y serán dos en una sola vida"* (Gén. 2,24) — ¿No es cierto que es una anticipación sorprendente haber encontrado esta *madurez* del hombre, esta verdadera *ruptura del cordón umbilical familiar* precisamente en el momento del matrimonio? — Otros verán en este texto, con razón, un momento de intensidad jurídica y aún política teniendo en cuenta el momento cultural en que se encuadra, una emancipación del *clan doméstico y familiar*. A nosotros interesa por encima de todas aquellas, también legítimas, interpretaciones, llegar a la primera, a la que está en la base de cualquier otra: la madurez *personal* de quien hace el matrimonio.

Y hay todavía más. El oráculo del Génesis afirma que *"serán dos en una sola vida"*[11]. En el texto sagrado no se advierte ninguna fusión en la cual alguna de los dos unidos pierda su propio identidad: serán todavía *dos* pero en *una* sola vida, en un sujeto nuevo de atribución lógica, de titularidad jurídica y social diverso del que se daba en su vida anterior. Sorprendámonos de nuevo en un contexto cultural de absoluta supremacía viril, de compraventa y atribución de la mujer de parte de los beduínos del desierto, de los patriarcas, de los reyes …

Desde el punto de vista de la Antropología estructural y cultural, esta *dualidad interpersonal* que con tanta finura descubrieron los griegos, los poetas del amor, atribuyéndola hasta una modalidad específica en la acción[12]; esta *dualidad* que es tan rica de dinamismo interno cuanto llena de tensiones y riesgos, llamada a desarrollarse en una intensidad y

---

[11] Es por demás reductivo limitar el sentido a la unión sexual como hacen los dos Códigos (cf. c. 1015 CIC 1917; c. 1061 CIC 1983).

[12] Es claro que nos referimos al *número dual* en especial como sujeto de la acción verbal. En el matrimonio por la singular interacción y complementariedad de los componentes del par se realiza sin duda la más cualificada expresión del *número dual*.

perpetuidad absolutas, en los altibajos de la pasión y del cansancio, es la humanísima grandeza y fragilidad cristiana y humana, del matrimonio.

"Simbiosis" suelen denominar los sicólogos aquel modo de existencia en pareja, en el cual uno de los componentes *da* y el otro sólo se *aprovecha* sin una propia contribución. Se trata ciertamente de una convivencia parasitaria. Pero no se necesita mucho para caer en la cuenta de que al menos semánticamente *simbiosis* no es sino la variante griega de la palabra, de origen latino, *convivencia* y que ésta a su vez no está lejana de las voces con amplia resonancia festiva y litúrgica que son *convivium, convite, consorcio* o *comunión.* La diferencia sin embargo entre una *simbiosis* enferma y una *simbiosis* sana y vivificante es la misma que la que existe entre egoísmo y amor. Idéntica a la que la tradición canónica, el Concilio y la norma vigente afirma existir — o deber ser — en el *darse y aceptarse los esposos mutuamente.* La sobrevivencia de los dos que permanecen unidos ayudándose a crecer, sin confundirse y menos aún fagocitarse.

No me resigno a dos nuevas digresiones — una poética, otra dolientemente real — para iluminar este misterio sublime que es el amor conyugal desde sus mismos principios.

La primera es une página de un libro muy leído hace algún tiempo, y que en el diálogo de dos jóvenes antes del matrimonio ha introducido dos citas llenas de belleza: *"Cuando nuestras dos almas se levanten unidas y fuertes, una frente a la otra, en silencio, siempre más juntas, hasta que sus alas, alargándose, se abrasen y ardan, ... habremos de buscar un lugar donde detenernos y amarnos por un día, mientras nos rodee la tiniebla y la hora de la muerte ... "* (Elizabet BARRETT): ¿Se puede pensar un modo más alto de expresar la perpetuidad, la entrega definitiva de un amor más fuerte que la muerte?

" ... To doy mi mano. Te doy mi amor más precioso que cualquier moneda. Te doy a mí mismo más allá de las prédicas y las leyes. ¿Quieres entregarte a mí tú misma? ¿Quieres venir a viajar conmigo? ¿Quieres que permanezcamos el uno junto al otro, unidos mientras nos quede un hálito de vida?" (Walt WHITMAN)[13] — He aquí en el latido del amor conyugal la fórmula viva del consentimiento matrimonial.

---

[13] Ambas citas están tomadas del conocidísimo 'Love Story' de E. SEGAL, c. XI.

Con la emoción de la poesía vivida y presenciada quiero añadir una anécdota de mi propia experiencia personal. Alvise Malatesta, un marido cualquiera de la humilde periferia romana, está enfermo con una grave crisis cardíaca. Cuando me lo comunica su esposa, Elsa Belfiore, me falta tiempo al día siguiente para ir a visitarlo al Hospital. Le digo que su esposa se siente muy sola. Y él con emoción observa: "*Es una mujer buenísima. Viene a verme todos los días y cuando por problemas con los trasportes públicos no puede llegar a tiempo siempre deja su paquetito al conserje para que me lo dé. Y este año cumpliremos los cincuenta de matrimonio ...*" Cuando al día siguiente comento la entrevista con la esposa y le expongo mi deseo y parecer de que su marido sanará; que haremos una fiesta maravillosa de sus bodas de oro, la mujer corta el vuelo de mi entusiasmo: "*Nada de fiesta. Alvise tiene un pésimo carácter y me ha hecho la vida muy difícil. Aunque esté años enteros en el Hospital iré a verle todos los días. Pero no quiero fiesta ninguna por haber hecho mi deber*" — Es cierto que añadir la nota 'conyugal' a la palabra amor puede ser a las veces desconcertante: pero estas historias de heroísmo cotidiano enseñan que querer el bien del otro/a más allá de todas las dificultades, aceptarlo como es y entregarse a él es una realización fuerte y sincera del consentimiento conyugal. Elsa y Alvise, Bellaflor y Malatesta, han muerto ya los dos: su vida al parecer común y áspera es un modelo también irrepetible de vivir hasta el final, un válido, validísimo consentimiento matrimonial.

Hemos vuelto a casa. Hemos reencontrado ese matrimonio tan bello como común y normal[14]. Pero ya es tiempo de ensayar otra de nuestras digresiones, tal vez de importancia mayor.

Sin pretensiones de análisis demasiado sutiles y completos, trataremos de deslindar alguna de las notas esenciales de la que hemos llamado '*personeidad*', con la que las personas realizan su pacto conyugal. Cierto serán aquellas que de alguna manera convengan a la finalidad de estas lecciones que, como queda dicho, no se proponen disertar sobre la persona y el mundo de lo personal, sino sobre el *matrimonio como acontecimiento personal e interpersonal y también personalizante*. Es posible que sutilizando más todavía, puesto que el consentimiento conyugal es un acto, no nos interese tanto el *ser* de la persona en sí, en su

---

[14] La analogía aquí cabría establecerla con la belleza limpia de las cosas más elementales: la piedra, el agua, el sol, la vida ...

infraestructura ontológica y metafísica, como su *acción* y en concreto ese acto complejo y existencial con el que se realiza la alianza esponsal.

Desde estas perspectivas me detendré especialmente en dos aspectos del ser dinámico personal — la *historicidad* y la *irrepetibilidad* — y en tres características del acto personal, aplicadas concretamente al que conocemos como consentimiento conyugal: la *totalidad*, la *autonomía* y la *comunicabilidad*. Creo que no estamos habituados a encontrar en nuestro Manuales tales palabras y ni siquiera tales ideas.

La *historicidad* de la persona es aquella característica por la que la persona se realiza a través de la actuación en el presente de toda su biografía pasada. Es este trazado en el tiempo el que dibuja su perfil existencial y la configura en cuanto tal. Y habría que añadir su futuro, su proyecto, presente en su *intención* punto de referencia esencial para el consentimiento conyugal[15]. Cualquiera que sea el valor que haya que atribuir a esta *historicidad* en todas las acciones humanas en general, no hay duda de que ella reviste la máxima importancia en las opciones *fuertes*, cual es la que lleva consigo la elección del matrimonio.

De la mano de la historicidad va la *irrepetibilidad* que no es sino una fenomenología de aquélla pero que en el estudio de *lo personal* adquiere un peculiar relieve. Porque introduce dos variantes metodológicas de interés: primero, nos hace extremar las cautelas cuando queremos reconocer en el esquema normativo la infinita e indefinible — ”*individuum ineffabile*”, lo individual, *a fortiori* lo *personal*, es indecible, decían en la Escuela — variedad de la personas; y además, porque en las acciones *personales* el *cómo* puede ser tan importante cuanto el *qué*, ya que puede suceder que sea precisamente el *cómo*, el modo, la cualidad de acción, la que comunique a ésta su fundamental *irrepetibilidad personal*[16].

Deteniéndonos ahora en las cualidades de la *acción personal*, reconozco como *totalidad*, la implicación de toda la persona en su acto; y en

---

[15] En función de la importancia destacada y determinante del consentimiento en el matrimonio, la intención ha adquirido desde siempre una importancia decisiva en la disciplina matrimonial canónica. Hasta el punto que bien podemos decir que es el nuestro el ordenamiento que mayor peso intencional — aun el el ámbito procesal, lo que es del todo singular e inexplicable sin recurrir a la naturaleza peculiar de nuestras normas — posee y conserva.

[16] Cf. SERRANO RUIZ, J.M., "La consideración existencial del matrimonio en la Causas canónicas de nulidad por incapacidad psíquica", en *Angelicum*, 68 (1991), 33-63; 173-229.

nuestro caso, en su *consentimiento conyugal*. De manera que bajo este aspecto considero del todo insuficiente, al menos en el sentido con que habitualmente se emplea, aplicar al consentimiento matrimonial el criterio habitual de entender y querer con que se mide la responsabilidad civil y penal genérica. Los textos conciliares y las normas que en ellos se inspiran insisten en una mutua donación y aceptación cordial y total que los esposos hacen mutuamente de sí mismos en el momento en que establecen su alianza conyugal[17]. Como tendremos ocasión de ver con más detalle dejar de lado — o en línea de capacidad o por limitación más o menos deliberada — aspectos como la afectividad, el amor, la disponibilidad, … puede incidir seriamente para hacer defectuosa hasta en su esencia esa acción personal y personalizante que es el pacto conyugal.

La *autonomía* es sin duda entre todas las características de la persona la que más y mejor la configura como tal ya desde la misma raíz semántica de la voz con que la designamos. Es sabido que el vocablo persona deriva de los juegos teatrales romanos en los que los actores usaban una máscara que llamaban *persona*. Ella servía para obviar la doble dificultad de no disponer de amplificadores técnicos y mecánicos de la voz y tampoco de la sofisticadas artes actuales del maquillaje. Se obtenían así las ventajas de mayor sonido y más eficaz caracterización en la recitación de las obras. Puesto que *persona* no se es sino cuando se está en condiciones de hablar fuerte y de poseer una voz y un papel en la comunidad humana, hemos de reconocer que si no antes al menos en el momento del matrimonio, los esposos han de estar en condiciones de obrar como *personas* con total autonomía y seriedad. De modo que exigir a la comunidad que escuche y respete su grave compromiso sea ciertamente comunicar carácter público a su opción — que lo tiene — que es no sólo personal, sino también socialmente trascendental y relevante. Bastaría pensar además al matrimonio como fiesta, como representación litúrgica en el sentido nobilísimo del *juego* que GUARDINI[18] advertía en las *funciones* sagradas para acabar de dar pleno sentido a una etimología muy afortunada por lo que hace al matrimonio. Y tanto ello es así que en una de mis decisiones se avanza la idea de que a la manera que la Iglesia ha acuñado el concepto y la expresión de *uso de razón* para recibir la Eucaristía, así se abra camino la de *uso de personalidad* como índice de madurez necesaria para celebrar el

---

[17] Cf. Const. Pastoral *Gaudium et Spes*, n. 48; *CIC* cc. 1055 y 1057.
[18] Cf. GUARDINI, R., *Lo spirito della Liturgia*, ed. it., Brescia, 1946, 65-81.

matrimonio[19]. Elegir con responsabilidad, aceptar con seriedad, cumplir con conciencia son sinónimos de asumir el matrimonio con verdadera autonomía.

Pues a la manera que la etimología de la palabra persona nos ayudaba a ahondar en lo personal, así el significado de la voz *autonomía* nos permite ahora penetrar en el núcleo esencial de la actitud del hombre creyente que celebra el matrimonio. El conoce el mensaje revelado expuesto por la Iglesia que mientras está en la Ley bien se puede reconocer como *heterónomo*. Pero como quiera que esa misma Ley le dice que su consentimiento es causa suficiente y necesaria del pacto, de algún modo ha de asumir *autonómamente* tal ley para hacerla ley propia por él querida, origen y manantial de *su matrimonio*.

Cuanto llevamos dicho en torno a la persona y a la acción personal se abre ahora a través de la *comunicabilidad* a una más estrecha relación con el matrimonio. Estamos habituados a considerar al hombre como un ser social. A entrever, como nuestro Hacedor, que *no es bueno que el hombre esté solo* (Gén. 2, 18). Las verdaderas acciones personales están abiertas a la comunicación. Y lo está sobre todo aquella por la que el hombre intenta poner fin a su individualidad, a su aislamiento, a su egoísmo, saciar su sed innata de dar y darse que figura entre sus más nobles tendencias innatas. A ella aludían nuestras primeras citas de los textos sagrados y de la inspiración poética.

La *interpersonalidad* asume y cualifica todas las características de lo personal enriqueciéndolas además con la mutua referencia del uno a la otra, como es necesario que exista en una unión tan intima y total como es el matrimonio. Presuponiendo, como hemos dicho, todas la características de la personeidad en lo interpersonal, hemos de referirnos a una que nace precisamente de esta interpersonalidad. Se trata de una esencial *relacionalidad* o *relatividad*[20] del matrimonio: característica todavía controvertida tanto en sus presupuestos como en su presentación

---

[19] Cf. una de 23 de mayo de 1980 en *Nulidad de Matrimonio coram Serrano*, Salamanca, 1981, 151-166, Original latino en *SRR Dec. seu Sent.*, 72 (1980), 366-378.

[20] Insisto en que las presentes reflexiones, como las lecciones que las desarrollarán, son propedéuticas; o si se quiere preambulares a cualquier consideración del matrimonio, en cualquiera de sus múltiples aspectos. Con todo de la *incapacidad relativa*, de sus planteamientos teóricos y del debate doctrinal en torno a ella tratan dos Sentencias c. SERRANO de 13 diciembre de 1991, ya citada (cf. supra, nota 3), y de 26 de marzo de 1993 (publicada en el *Anuario Argentino de Derecho Canónico*, 1 (1994), 157-174).

existencial, pero que a mi modo de ver es fundamental en el reconocimiento de la genuina esencia del matrimonio. La *dualidad* penetra de tal modo la esencia del matrimonio que excluirla en cuanto tal parece un contrasentido. Y por tanto es perfectamente legítimo admitir que las razones de ser o no ser del matrimonio tanto pueden deducirse de cada uno de los cónyuges como de la relación en si misma. No podemos entretenernos en la exposición detallada de la *relatividad* en la consideración canónica del matrimonio[21]. Pero sí quisiera salir al paso de dos cuestiones: una de método y otra de fondo.

Se podría objetar que este planteamiento lleva consigo la adopción de la ideología existencialista en el tratamiento del matrimonio en el ordenamiento canónico. Pero creo que escrutar todos los aspectos de la realidad sin comprometer los principios esenciales que orientan la investigación, justifican el empleo de métodos que no requieren por fuerza estar de acuerdo en todo o en parte con los principios ideológicos de los autores que los han propuesto.

La segunda cuestión presentaría el problema de si una propuesta como la *relatividad* en el matrimonio no atenta a la identidad inmutable del pacto, a la esencialidad de sus propiedades, a la irrenunicabilidad de sus finalidades ... Después de cuanto llevamos dicho en torno a las características esenciales de lo *personal* y de su fenomenología, surge espontánea la pregunta de si no será precisamente en esta existencialidad en la consideración del matrimonio en la que se salva su núcleo real más allá de las especulaciones abstractas de la teoría. Centrarnos en la consideración existencial del caso concreto en especial en lo que concierne a la relación entre las personas que son sus protagonistas y a las circunstancias en que se desarrolla su relación, no es sino someter al contraste del modelo normativo la vida misma[22].

Es posible que haya llegado la hora de regresar definitivamente a casa después de estas sabrosas digresiones sobre la esencia misma del

---

[21] Está en trance de publicación, bajo los auspicios de la Facultad de Derecho Canónico de la Universidad Pontifícia de Salamanca, un artículo sobre 'La incapacidad relativa en el can. 1095, 3' (cf. *Actas del XIII Simposio sobre Derecho procesal y matrimonial Canónico*, Santiago de Compostela, septiembre 1995).

[22] También el matrimonio, como suele decirse de la decisión judicial, tiene dos momentos: uno doctrinal, teórico, modélico y otro encarnado, existencial, concreto. De este último se trata de reconocer si *realiza* o no aquellas notas esenciales, que, evidentemente, no puede acoger en su ser principios abstractos.

matrimonio. Y sentados ya en paz en nuestro hogar de siempre, tratar de responder a una última inquietud de nuestros hermanos mayores y ya no tanto: se trata de la tensión entre *persona* e *instituto* relevante en el matrimonio como en tantos otros campos de nuestra difícil era, cargada de riesgo y de esperanza.

¿Matrimonio personal, interpersonal, existencial o matrimonio esencial, inconmovible, institucional? Pero, ¿por qué no un matrimonio instituto personal e interpersonal? Con todas la consecuencias que la síntesis lleve consigo de una y otra parte.

Desde el comienzo de estas páginas se ha insistido en su finalidad integrativa más que disociativa y mucho menos polémica. Hemos reconocido en el mundo de la persona y de lo personal un punto de referencia para la sensibilidad actual y por tanto capaz de revitalizar hoy la imagen de matrimonio cristiano de siempre. Creemos también que la palabra y el concepto de 'instituto' en el Derecho es desmesuradamente amplio hasta el punto de arriesgar una cierta equivocidad en una realidad tan auténtica y única que invalida todas las analogías, como es el matrimonio. Es cierto que hablar de *instituto personal e interpersonal* todavía no transmite con la debida precisión la exigente identidad del pacto conyugal. Pero sin duda que lleva a prestar más atención e importancia a aspectos y consecuencias que hasta ahora han sido mantenidos demasiado al margen. Como creo que hemos tenido ocasión de comprobar en estos días en los que hemos hablado del núcleo esencial de la familia entre los muros cálidos y amigos de nuestro hogar universitario.

Mons. José María Serrano Ruiz
Auditor de la Rota Romana.

THE PERSONAL CHARACTER OF MARRIAGE.
A SWING OF THE PENDULUM

Right from the very beginning I would like to explain that we will not deal concretely with some of the issues which are determined by legal theory and canonical jurisprudence about marriage — although it would be indispensible to deal with them — but we will deal with a way of presentation or presupposition which is common to all of them. So, therefore, we will prove the utility of this lecture, but it will be a different kind of utility than one which can be derived from a single concrete point. I am also aware that this is a university or doctoral work: therefore, it is different from one which should be done when dealing with a sententia or pronouncement in a given judicial case. As a result, we have a broader perspective on certain aspects, which in the beginning may seem abstract; in fact these are necessary presuppositions for a bigger and better existential analysis of the cases which we have before us. There will be a sort of paradox in these words. As I have already said, they are intended to be general principles, fundamental truths; but on the other hand I would like them to be full of existentialism, of faithfulness to real life, even if we have to move further away from abstraction. Thus in other words: this is a speculation at the service of real facts.

I want to prevent you from having another possible misunderstanding. The misunderstanding is that we must be intransigent in principle and reject immediately as heterodoxy anyone who holds different principles. I think that it does not have to be this way, and this could not be further from our intentions. I think that these ideas, although I know they may be different from our daily perspectives, do fit with the principles we referred to, and they entail a complementarity rather than a contrast. They are meant to illumine aspects which until now have not been explored too much, and are not meant to tear down the former principle, but rather to offer a global point of view.

I am not trying to be revolutionary in these ideas but to illuminate aspects about the conjugal agreement which will be useful not only in the juridical-canonical consideration, but also will spill over into dogmatic, moral, pastoral, etc., dimensions[1]. It is necessary to touch on fundamental points which have repercussions in the canonical vision of marriage and also on the causes of the nullity of marriage, in as much as they imply the existence or non-existence of matrimony. I want to avoid an excessive analysis of the core and essence of canonical marriage, and avoid a methodology that excessively analyzes the Christian mystery. Normally we are used to a methodological analysis of norms that presupposes the natural law and the bond of marriage[2]. I am not going to do that. It is true that with the analysis, a very detailed analysis, we can arrive at didactic and normative reasonings: but we also run the risk of overlooking the fundamental aspects of the institution of marriage.

I will give you an example to which we will return later: up to now, who has invested time seriously in studying the dual nature of marriage in its sacramental aspect? For who has been able to understand the transcendence implied in the fact that marriage has a dual nature — which presupposes that in the economy of salvation, all the sacraments are unipersonal (require only one person), and presupposes that marriage requires two persons, consisting of both the communion and the consent?[3] And thus other aspects can be achieved.

Let us allow ourselves some digressions from the normal way we develop our colloquial canons and professional conversations, and let us attempt to move to a different level of thinking, which is more like looking down at a turbulent river, through which it is not easy to wade. This is the point where the canonical study of marriage finds its source. But let us not forget that we have to return home to the secure and ever-constant place which is the marriage institution, which the Church looks after with such diligence and care.

First of all it is important to make a point about the *uniqueness* which is proper to marriage. Not only because this is the almost exclusive concern about marriages which come to our tribunals, but also because its

---

[1] Cf. SERRANO RUIZ, J.M., "El carácter personal del matrimonio: presupuestos y perspectivas para las Causas canónicas de nulidad" in *Iustus Iudex,* Festgabe für Paul Wesemann, Essen, Ludgerus-Verlag, 1990, 310-329.

[2] The observation is especially applicable for canon 1095 ff., dealing in a detailed way with fundamental aspects of the human act (personal).

[3] Cf. a Sentence c. SERRANO, from 13 December 1991 in *SRR Dec. seu Sent.,* 83 (1991), 756-787.

juridical identity is different from any other thing.[4] This is true to such an extent that I think one can say that I will not make digressions away from marriage but within marriage itself. The digressions will introduce us into the heart of the matter: to talk about the heart of the matter is an appropriate metaphor to be applied to the Christian mystery of love. This is the case concerning many other situations which are not explored much, although logically it would have been better to start there. In any case, we should not feel isolated or humble in our work on marriage. For after being familiar with the Gospel for a long time, I realized that there is a great paradox hidden in the beginning of the parable of the Good Samaritan concerning the doctor of the Law who comes to Jesus and asks the question about the path to salvation. And the Teacher responds by using a mayeutical (Socratic) method intended to challenge the one who asks the question: What is written in the Law? And the teacher responds with the letter of the Law. The prophet encourages him. And the inquisitive man asks for another way out. Who is my neighbor? It seems to me that the introduction to this story would have been much larger: How are you as the Teacher of the Law not able to recognize the second meaning of the Law? In other words, we will be in a difficult situation if we seriously try to define the essence (fundamental core) of marriage. There was a very distinguished countryman of yours who wrote in his fundamental work, that the strange destiny of the most important realities of man is that these realities are only accessible to human experience, and not to rational description.[5] We have not had a true experience of this fundamental reality of marriage; probably nobody has had this. We can however make an attempt to express it in a sort of logical formula which may seem adequate. Nevertheless, we should not overlook the fact that it is important to try to grasp this fundamental aspect of marriage.[6]

After these preliminary observations, we can return to our title, "Reflections on the personal character of marriage". Concerning this title, I want to express some doubts about the concepts I am using. For

---

[4] Cf. SERRANO RUIZ, J.M., *Acerca de algunas notas específicas del derecho y deber conyugal,* in *Revista Española de Derecho Canónico,* 85 (1974), 5 ss.

[5] Cf. MOELLER, CH., *Literatura del siglo XX y Cristianismo,* Spanish edition, Madrid, 1955, Volume II, 360.

[6] It will be appropriate to make a comparison with what the First Vatican Council says about the human intellect, namely, that you'll never be able to exhaust the mysteries of faith, but that the attempt itself may be fruitful (cf. DENZINGER, *Enchiridion Symbolorum,* n. 1796).

instance, the word 'character'. Probably someone else would have pre-
ferred *'indole'* (nature) or 'kind'. But the word *'indole'* looks to me as if
it is too literally translated from the Latin and too general; it is then perhaps related to 'person' rather than to 'personal' — 'personal nature'?
Absolutely not, it can only be acceptable in the metaphysical meaning as
a synonym of essence; but in this way it would somehow suggest the
idea that we want to remove the idea that objective reality does not exist.
And yet this reality is still physical, in the essential core of marriage,
different even from the persons themselves who are the spouses. Why
then not use the term, 'personal essence of marriage'? The difficulties
arise from the other side — too much abstraction; almost to the point of
contradiction with the concept itself of 'person' and 'personhood',
devoid of all existential meaning. 'Personal vision', then? Certainly not;
it will lead us not to take this seriously, and we could appear subjective.
And if in the beginning we might have been subjective, nonetheless we
intend to reach the very core of the problem.

Therefore, 'character'. This word embraces all the weight of the clas-
sical meanings, histories, and even grammatical, cultural, anthropologi-
cal, and psychological meanings that are contained within. Yet, when we
use the term 'character', we want to show a word that exhibits in the
deepest way the mode of being a reality. And at the same time we want
to distinguish it from any other reality and identify the reality in an
unequivocal way. And when such an essential core is identifiable as a
complex whole not easily determined, we need to take into account all
the components to reach the most exact idea of character that is possible,
of the formality that we speak of, that makes it to be what it is.

Therefore, 'personal'. The relevance of the 'person' and of the 'personal' is certainly not a conquest or a sign of progress in the renewed
vision of marriage. It is first of all a 'sign of the times' that is mani-
fested in everything: in public and private law, in constitutional law,
of the internal and international spheres, in the Church — in Churches —
and in civil society. It is more a common and total inspiration
than one norm or combination of norms around a concrete juridical
institution. It becomes even more urgent than logical in those spaces
of psychology, of morality, of sociology, or of law in which the
human person occupies the position of greatest leadership. It would be
incorrect to maintain that it is only in marriage that the Church meets
the opportunity of welcoming and developing this movement, as the

splendid Pastoral Constitution *Gaudium et Spes* of the Second Vatican Council, not to mention the other council documents, have inspired us to accept. That inspiration is our point of departure. Marriage is an application, which is very opportune considering everything we have been saying about law, which concerns more immediately the human being and his world.

Of course we cannot go here into detail about all the recent intellectual speculation and all the literature concerning the 'person' and the 'personal'.[7] Yet, it also interests me to distinguish the fact — following in the commentary of our title — that we have spoken of 'personal' character and not 'personalist'. The expression 'personalist' is normally invoked when people refer to marriage in two different contexts: or, in the first place, in relation to the long-ago controversy between 'personalist' purposes and 'institutional' purposes which had their most well-known and censured representative in H. Doms[8]; or the second contrasting view which can be called an institutionalist conception — which also in this case would be better referred to, I think, as institutional — also with reference to marriage[9]. But our use of the expression 'personal' — 'personal' character; rather than 'personalist' or 'personalistic' — attempts to emphasize the integrated aspects and not the disassociative ones between for instance persona and institution, or between human and personal. These are realities which do not exlcude one another. A person does not try to deny one in order to reaffirm the other; but we want to dig into both aspects to enrich them and make them mutually safe, because they are both present in Christian marriage. We will not weaken 'personal' to the point of reducing it into an indifferentiated individualism; neither do we exalt the term institutional to the extent that we make it insensible to the personal; but we recognize in all human beings the undeniable prerogatives of 'personeidad' (personhood) in agreement with the happy expression of my countryman,

---

[7] Cf. "El caracter personal del matrimonio", cit., in *Iustus Iudex,* p. 311, n. 2.

[8] Cf. *Vom Sinn und Zweck der Ehe. Eine systematische Studie,* Breslau, 1935, *AAS* 36 (1944), 103.

[9] There have been several attempts to use the concept and terminology of *juridical institution* in order to avoid the expression of *contract*, which has been applied to marriage and of which we all know it is very unfortunate. Precisely because the concept of *institution* is so extensive, this attempt can result in frustration. Is it not true that a contract is an institution? As we have said, it is important to explain marriage from the perspective of marriage itself and not from perspectives of other figures, no matter how many similarities that they may have with marriage.

X. Zubiri's philosophy[10], and in the marriage institution we will
acknowledge that there are the most noble origins and the highest final-
ities which make it innate and inherent to the human person.

In our severe limits, not trying to be intransigent nor tedious, in our
digressions on the logical and cultural principles of marriage, let us now
look at the Word of God, the Anthropology and the Law on the occasion
of the personhood of marriage.

It is difficult to walk quickly through the whole of Revelation. And
this is even more so because marriage is one of the themes which runs
through the whole message of God to humanity since the origins of creation up through the royal Wedding of the Bride and the Lamb. But it
may help to make, in an emblematic phrase, a concrete interpretation of
the words from Genesis: "Therefore a man will leave his father and
his mother, and be united with his wife, and the two will be one life."
(Genesis 2:24) Is it not true that it is surprising to find this human maturity, namely, this rupture, precisely at the moment of marriage? Some
will see in this text, with reason, a moment of juridical and even politi-
cal intensity, taking into account the cultural moment in which it is
found, an emancipation of the familiar and domestic clan.

We are interested in arriving at the first interpretation which is at the
basis of all the interpretations which can be considered: namely, the personal maturity of the one who enters marriage. And there is yet more.
The prophecy of Genesis affirms that "they will be two in one life."[11] In
the sacred text, we do not find a union in which either of the two who
are united loses his/her identity. They will still be two, but in one life; in
a new logic of subjective thinking, in a new juridical and social title, and
different from the one in which they were previously. We come again
upon this reality in the cultural context of absolute male supremacy, of
the buying and selling of women on the part of the Bedouins of the
desert, of the patriarchs, of the kings.

From a perspective of structural and cultural Anthropology, this is an
interpersonal duality which with such refinement was discovered by the
Greeks, the poets of love. They attributed it to a special modality in the

---

[10] Cf. ZUBIRI, X., *Sobre la esencia,* Madrid, 1962, 504-505.
[11] It is useless to limit the meaning to sexual union as they do in the two Codes
(cf. c. 1015 CIC 1917; c. 1061 CIC 1983).

action[12]; this duality which is so rich in internal dynamism and at the same time is full of tensions and risks, is called to develop in absolute intensity and perpetuity, then in the ups and downs of passion and boredom. It is the great humanity and fragility, Christian and human, of marriage.

Psychologists used to call that way of life 'symbiosis', in which one of the partners takes advantage of the other without contributing anything. Certainly it is a parasitical way of living. But it does not take long to realize that at least semantically a symbiosis is just a Greek variation of the word of Latin origin — conviviency — and that this word itself is not far from the concepts 'convivium', 'convite', 'consortio' and 'communion', which contain a liturical and festive meaning. The difference, however, between a sick symbiosis, and a healthy and living symbiosis, is the same as the one existing between egotism and love. This is identical to the canonical tradition, the Council and the present norms which affirm that there exists, in this life together, a mutual acceptance of the spouses. The survival of the two who stay united help each other to grow, without confusing and tearing each other down or harming each other.

I still continue with new digressions, one poetic and the other sadly real, to illuminate this sublime mystery which is conjugal love from its origins.

The first is a page from a book which was widely read some time ago, and which in the dialogue of the young before marriage has introduced these two quotes full of beauty: "When our two souls are elevated in unity and power, facing each other, in silence, but together always, until their wings stretch themselves and embrace and consume, we should seek a place to stay together and love each other for a day, while darkness is around us and the hour of death … " (Elizabeth Barrett). Can you think of a better way to express the perpetuity, the definitive surrender of love, stronger than death?

" … I give you my hand. I give you my love more precious than any money. I give you myself beyond all the preaching and laws. Do you

---

[12] It is clear that we refer to the two of them, especially as the subject of the verbal action. In marriage, in order for there really to be a oneness and a mutuality between the two, we use the more qualified expression of the two of them.

wish to give yourself to me? Do you want to travel with me? Do you want to remain as one joined to the other, united while we have a breath of life?" (Walt Whitman)[13] Here you have a heartbeat pulsing with conjugal love, the living formula of matrimonial consent.

With the emotion of such a poetic experience as quoted above, I want to add a story of my own personal experience. Alvise Malatesta, a husband of the suburbs of Rome, is sick with a serious heart attack. When his wife Elsa Belfiore tells me about this, I do not have the time to visit them till the following day. I tell him that his wife feels very lonely. And with emotion he observes: "She is a very good woman. She comes to see me every day and because of problems with public transportation, she arrives late and always leaves a present for the cleaning person, and he gives it to me. And this year we will celebrate our 50th wedding anniversary ... " When on the following day I comment the conversation with his wife and tell her that I think her husband will recover, and that in the future we will prepare a wonderful party for the golden anniversary, his wife stops my enthusiasm: "No celebration at all. Alvise has a bad character and he has made my life very difficult. And for years he has been in the hospital and I go to see him every day. But I do not want a party because I am doing my duty." It is true that to add the word 'conjugal' to the other word love can be disconcerting: but these stories of daily heroism teach us to want the good of the other despite all the difficulties, to accept the person as she/he is. To give one's self to the other is a sincere and strong realization of the conjugal consent. Elsa and Alvise, Belfiore and Malatesta, have both died. Their life which may look common and hard, is also an unforgettable, unique model of living till the end a very valid marriage consent.

We returned home. We have met again this marriage so beautiful as well as so common and normal.[14] But it is now time to work out another digression of sometimes greater importance.

Without pretentions of a too subtle and complete analysis, we derive one of the essential connotations of that essential word we call *personhood*, with which persons achieve their conjugal bond. It is true that they will be some of those which somehow converge or are in accordance

---

[13] Both quotes are taken from the well-known 'Love Story' by E. SEGAL, c. XI.
[14] It could be appropriate to make the analogy with the clear beauty of the most elementary things: rock, water, sun, life ...

with the finality of this lecture, which, as already said, does not try to speculate on the person and the world of the personal, but rather on the marriage as personal and interpersonal, and also as a personalizing event. It is possible to make a more subtle analysis. However, we are not interested in the *being* of the person itself, namely in its ontological and metaphysical infrastructure, but more so in its action and in the concrete, in that complex and existential act through which the marriage agreement is achieved.

From these perspectives I will discuss into detail two aspects of the dynamic-personal being — namely, historicity and irrepeatibility — and also three characteristics of the personal act, which are applied concretely to what we know as matrimonial consent, namely totality, autonomy and communicability. I believe that we are not used to finding these words in our manuals, nor even such ideas.

The *historicity* of the person is that characteristic by which the person finds his/her realization through his action in the present of all his/her past biography. It is this characteristic which draws his/her existential form, and shapes it as such. And it will be good to add his future project, which is present as his intention, as an essential point of reference for the matrimonial consent.[15] Whatever the value is, we have to attribute to this historicity in all human actions in general; there is no doubt that it has the greatest importance in decisive options, such as the one which implies the decision of marriage.

Joining hands with historicity is *uniqueness*, which is nothing less than a phenomenology of the former, but which in the study of the personal, acquires a particular relevance. Because it introduces us to methodological variations of interest: first, it urges us to be careful when we are trying to recognize in the normative scheme the infinite and personal individual. "The ineffable individual", the individual, *a fortiori* the personal are indescribable, as they used to say in school (a variety of persons). This is so also because in the personal actions the *how* can be as important as the *what*. Given the fact that it is

---

[15] In the light of the explicit and determinant role of the consensus in marriage, the intention has always acquired a strong importance in the discipline of marriage law. We could even say that our vision on marriage law today attributes an even bigger importance to the intention, even in the field of process law, which is singular and unexplicable, without emphasizing the specific nature of our norms.

precisely the *how*, the mode, the quality of the action, the one which communicates to the individual (or person) its fundamental personal uniqueness.[16]

We now consider the qualities of *personal action*, I acknowledge as a *totality*, the implication of the whole person in his/her act, and in the case we are dealing with, his/her matrimonial consent. From this perspective, hence, I consider it insufficient, at least in the common way we use it, to apply to the matrimonial consent the normal criteria of understanding and desiring with which civil and penal responsibility is measured. The Conciliar texts, and the legislative norms which receive their inspiration from them, insist on a mutual donation and cordial and total acceptance which the spouses give of themselves at the moment of establishing their marriage bond.[17] As we will later see with some detail, to overlook aspects such as affectivity, love and receptivity, can have a serious impact on making the marriage bond defective, even in its essence as a personal and personalizing action.

Autonomy is without question the characteristic which most forms the person, among all the characteristics which make up a person, as we have already established, and considering the semantic meaning we are using. It is well known that the word person is derived from the Roman plays at the theater, in which the actors used a mask which they called "persona". This mask was helpful to overcome the double difficulty of not having microphones for the voice, and also not having the sophisticated make-up which we have today. Using the "persona" gave them the advantages of better quality sound, and better characterization in the reciting of the script. Given the fact that one is a person only when one is capable of speaking out loud, and when one possesses a voice and a role in the human community — we must acknowledge that before the marriage vows are given, the spouses have to be capable of acting as persons with total autonomy and seriousness. Accordingly, to ask the community to witness and respect their sharing of vows, also communicates a public character to their decision, which is not only personal but also socially relevant and transcendental. It will be sufficient to think of marriage as a feast, as a liturgical representation in the novel sense of the

---

[16] Cf. SERRANO RUIZ, J.M., "La consideración existencial del matrimonio en las Causas canónicas de nulidad por incapacidad psíquica", in *Angelicum*, 68 (1991), 33-63; 173-229.

[17] Cf. Pastoral Constitution *Gaudium et Spes*, n. 48, and *CIC* cc. 1055-1057.

play which Guardini[18] found in the sacred functions in order to give total meaning to an etymology in reference to marriage. This is accurate so much so that, in one of my decisions, I suggest that there is a similarity between the way that the Church uses the expression *use of reason* which is required before one may receive the Eucharist, and the *use of personality*, which is what the Church requires before one may validly contract marriage.[19] To choose in a responsible way, and to accept and live up to responsibilities, are ways of saying that a person enters marriage with true autonomy.

In the same way that the etymology of the word "person" helps us to dig into the personal, the meaning behind the concept *autonomy* allows us to penetrate into the essential core of a believer who enters marriage. He/she knows the revealed message exposed by the Church and meanwhile is part of the law which can be recognized as *heteronomous*. But because this same law tells him/her that the consent is a sufficient and necessary cause of the marriage bond, somehow the individual must assume in an autonomous way such law, in order to assimilate the law, which is the origin and foundation of marriage.

All that we have said so far about the person, and personal action, is now apparent, in our presenting the idea that *communicability* is in a very close relationship with marriage. We are used to thinking of the human person as a social being. And to accept, as our Creator does, that it is not good that the human person is alone. The real personal actions are open to communication. It is especially clear that the personal action through which a person intends to put an end to his individuality, his isolation, egotism, happens when he quenches the innate human desire to give himself to another. This desire is one of the human being's most noble innate tendencies. Our first quotations of the sacred texts, and the poetic inspiration, alluded to this personal action.

The "interpersonality" assumes and qualifies all the characteristics of the personal enriching them with mutual reference to each other, as it is required that they do exist in a union as intimate and total as marriage is. Presupposing, as we have said, all the characteristics of personality in the interpersonal, we should refer to one of them which derives from this

---

[18] Cf. GUARDINI, R., *Lo spirito della Liturgia*, Italian edition, Brescia, 1946, 65-81.

[19] Cf. one from 23 May 1980 in *Nulidad de Matrimonio coram Serrano*, Salamanca, 1981, 151-166. Original Latin in *SRR, Dec. seu Sent.*, 72 (1980), 366-378.

interpersonality.[20] Namely it concerns the essential *relational meaning* or *relative character* of marriage: a characteristic which is still controversial in its presuppositions as well as in its existential presentation, but which in my opinion is fundamental in the acknowledgement of the real essence of marriage. The "duality" penetrates in such a way the essence of marriage that if we excluded it as such, marriage would become senseless. Nevertheless, it is perfectly legitimate to admit that the reasons for the existence or non-existence of a marriage can be deduced from both of the spouses, and also from the relationship itself. We cannot give a detailed exposition of the relative character of mariage in its canonical consideration[21]. But nevertheless I would like to deal with two questions: one of method and one of content.

Some people may object that this way of presenting the issue implies the existential ideology in the treatment of marriage in the canonical order. But I believe that to scrutinize all the aspects of this reality without compromising the essential principles that give direction to the study, justifies methods that do not necessarily require agreement in all or in part with the ideological principles of the authors who proposed them.

The second question presents the problem, concerning whether the relative character in marriage tries to oppose the immutable nature of the bond, or the essence of its properties, or the permanence of its ends. After all we have said about the essential characteristics of the person and its phenomenology, the spontaneous question comes up that precisely considers existentialism in marriage, in which its essential core is preserved because it goes beyond abstract speculations of theory. To center ourselves on the existential consideration of the concrete case is to submit to a contradiction of the normative way of life itself. This is especially true concerning the relationship between the persons who are the protagonists in marriage, and the circumstances in which their relationship develops.[22]

---

[20] I insist that present reflections are only basic, in relationship to more detailed reflections. In a more detailed way, *relative incapacity* is written up in two sentences, c. Serrano of 13 December 1991, already cited (cf. above, note 3), and of 26 March 1993 (published in *Anuario Argentino de Derecho Canónico*, 1 (1994), 157-174.)

[21] There is at the present moment, under the auspices of the Faculty of Canon Law of the Pontifical University of Salamanca, going to be published an article about "La incapacidad relative en el can. 1095.3" (cf. *Actas del XIII Simposio sobre Derecho procesal y matrimonial Canónico*, Santiago de Compostela, September 1995).

[22] Marriage also, as has been said in a judicial decision, has two moments, one doctrinal and theoretical; and the other incarnate, existential, concrete. Of this last, we try

It is possible that it is time now to come back home, after having had these nice digressions about the essence of marriage itself. And we feel now settled peacefully in our home; we will try to respond to a last question of our elder brothers which deals with the tension between "person" and "institution"; this is relevant in marriage as in so many other fields in our difficult time, which is full of both risk and hope.

Personal marriage, interpersonal, existential or essential marriage, immutable, institutional? But, why then not an institutional marriage, personal and interpersonal? With all the consequences of a synthesis, which can take the side of one or the other part.

Since the beginning of these pages we have insisted on the integrative finality of marriage, rather than on a dissociative one, and even less a polemical one. We have recognized in the world of the person and of the personal a point of reference for the current sensibility, and therefore we want to revitalize today the longstanding image of Christian marriage. We also believe that the word and the concept of "institution" in Law is too wide, to the extent that it risks making a certain equivocation in a reality as authentic and unique that it invalidates all analogies, such as is the case with marriage. It is true that the fact of speaking of "personal and interpersonal institution" still does not translate with appropriate precision the demanding nature of the marital bond. But without question, it lends more attention and importance to aspects and consequences that until now have been supported only marginally. Just as we have had an occasion to speak during these days, of the essential core of marriage, here in the warm confines and among friends of our university home.

Msgr. José María Serrano Ruiz
Auditor of the Roman Rota.

Translation by Michael Bradley and Jesús Castillo-Coronado.

---

to recognize whether those other essential statements are accomplished or not; evidently, they cannot be accepted as abstract principles.

CATHOLIC IDENTITY OF
HEALTHCARE INSTITUTIONS
IN A TIME OF CHANGE

Introduction

It is indeed a great honour for me to have been invited to take part in the annual Msgr. W. Onclin Chair, and, more particularly to be able to share a platform with Msgr. José M. Serrano Ruiz, one of the most respected of the Rotal judges, and a priest who has profoundly influenced the practice of church tribunals by his insistence on the dignity of the human person and the interpersonal communication that is required in marriage.

I would like to take this opportunity to thank the organizers, and in particular dr. Rik Torfs, Dean of the Faculty of Canon Law, for their kind and most gracious hospitality and I wish them every succes in their endeavours.

I hope that what I will speak of here this afternoon will not only be helpful, but will also be useful to you. For, today I would like to address one special dimension of the Church's apostolic activity: its healthcare ministry, to note some of the challenges it faces in a time of rapid change. You will not be surprised, I hope, if I operate more from a North American perspective. While I have been privileged at times to help look at this issue in other parts of the world, particularly in Ireland, Australia and New Zealand, my experience is mostly limited to the North American scene, covering both Canada and the United States. However, as I look at other issues that the Church has had to face recently — such as that of clerical sexual abuse — I realize that what is an issue in one part of the Church can easily become such elsewhere within a very short period of time. For this reason, I hope that some of the points I will raise today will also be of help to those in Europe who are called upon to advise bishops and religious leaders in matters relating to choices to be taken in furthering the healthcare mission of the Church.

Throughout the centuries, the Catholic Church has been identified with the healing mission of Christ[1]. From very early times — even in the Acts of the Apostles (see Acts, 3, 1-10, etc.) — we have noted a concern for healing of the sick, for the wellbeing of the total person, and for good health in general. Today, it is recognized that the Catholic Church, with its general and acute-care hospitals, out-patient services, clinics, rehabilitation centres, homes for the elderly, hospices, and so forth, is the largest provider of healthcare in the world. The Church feels called to this ministry, not because of the power or control that it affords, but rather because it follows the teaching of Jesus: "Whatever you did to the least of these my brothers, you did unto me" (Mt. 25, 40). The example of the Good Samaritan as proposed in the parable has been with us since the very beginning of the Church (Lk. 10, 33) and has guided our activities. The Church certainly has no intention of giving up or relinquishing this apostolate — the recent establishment, on February 11, 1985, of the Pontifical Council for Healthcare is a good example of this resolve[2] — but, nevertheless, the Church must face new challenges arising not only from the marketplace, but also from advances in medical science and from a new understanding of health itself.

In recent years, the focus has shifted from illness and healing to wellness and health. This entails an entirely new approach to an apostolate that was well established and firmly set in its ways. The shift to preventative measures, and away from healing, has necessarily changed the way in which the Church seeks to foster the well-being of all persons. It is much less expensive to provide immunization to children than to have to care for them for years afterwards; the same could also be said for good prenatal care. New emphasis placed on personal health-giving habits (for instance, in relation to smoking and alcohol abuse) will help diminish the need for extensive hospitalization in years ahead. Such a shift in emphasis, however, puts into question the large institutions we sponsor and the number of persons actively employed in them.

One further source of change is the focus now placed on collaborative efforts. Rather than having each institution — hospital, clinic, hospice, home for the elderly, and so forth — working on its own and offering

---

[1] For instance, the continued presence of various hospitaller Orders, such as the Order of Malta, is indicative of this fact.

[2] See *Annuario Pontificio*, 1995, 1750.

duplicated services, these various works are now being grouped together in systems, alliances, joint ventures and similar undertakings, both in an effort to reduce costs, but also, and even more importantly, to provide a continuum of care, from conception to the grave. The organization of what we have come to call "integrated delivery units" (or similar under- takings) has enabled us to follow a person throughout the course of life, and adopt a holistic perspective on that person's health. However, in many cities and towns, the Catholic Church is not able to provide all the components required for a truly integrated delivery unit — pre- and neo-natal care, obstetrics, pediatrics, family and internal medicine, gerontology, hospices, and so forth — and thus has had to enter into col- laborative ventures with other providers, many of whom are not Catholic, or even religious in nature for that matter. This coming together with secular undertakings has raised new problems that were not foreseen even fifteen years ago. To what extent can a Catholic insti- tution collaborate with another entity that not only does not espouse Catholic values, but even at times is militantly working against them? I am thinking in particular of issues relating to conception and birth (with abortion a major factor) and to death and dying with dignity (of which euthanasia is becoming a prime element).

In view of this, we must study carefully what we mean by the Catholic identity of our institutions and activities, and then determine how we can preserve and even enhance this identity in the years ahead.

It must be said right from the beginning that we are dealing with a *process*, not with a cut and dry situation. As life evolves, so too do the medical techniques and the business practices applied to our everyday situations. As with other areas of church life and practice, we do not pretend to have all the answers; indeed, if we did, there would be no need to study the questions further. Some of the answers that shall be proposed might eventually be found to be wrong, or not complete; some might even produce negative effects rather than the hoped-for ones that humanity is desperately seeking. The approval of the drug thalidomide some thirty or so years ago is an excellent example of this: while the immediate effects were considered to be quite benefi- cial, the long-term ones were disastrous. It is very consoling also to note that the Church has to update its teachings continually. The exam- ple of the teaching on the death penalty found in the *Catechism of the*

Catholic Church[3] and the revised teaching put forward by pope John Paul II some three years later in the encyclical *Evangelium vitae*[4] is an excellent example of this type of development. For these reasons, and in this evolving context, I would like to look today at three major points: what constitutes the catholic identity of any institution; what constitutes the catholic identity of a healthcare institution; what are some of the major challenges facing catholic healthcare these days and how can we respond to them.

I. The Catholic Identity of an Institution

The Code of Canon Law does not specifically and directly continue the criteria for catholic identity. So, we must proceed by analogy (canon 19). But, in addition, we must recognize that there are many ways of approaching the issue of catholic identity: we can take a purely legal or "institutional" approach, using verifiable criteria and principles to determine what we could call "catholicity"[5]; or we can take a more doctrinal approach, focussing our attention on what we could call "ecclesiality"; or we could even proceed from a mixture of the two, as Pope John Paul II in the Apostolic Constitution *Ex corde Ecclesiae*[6]. There is also a fourth possible way, by identifying values that we wish to promote and by observing them.

a. Institutional or legal criteria

Obviously, canonists and other lawyers prefer the legal or "catholicity" aproach because it is clear and precise. They also like the hierarchical dimension found in it because it establishes clear lines of responsibility. However, we must keep in mind that there is more to the life of the Church than simply law and institutions. Law presupposes faith and commitment. Otherwise, it is of little avail[7].

---

[3] See *Catechism of the Catholic Church*, No 2267. See also: "On file", in *Origins*, 24 (1994-1995), 692: "The discussion of the death penalty in the new Catechism of the Catholic Church will be revised to reflect the stronger reservation expressed by Pope John Paul II on this topic in his encyclical, 'The Gospel of Life', said Cardinal Joseph Ratzinger" (March 30, 1995).

[4] See JOHN PAUL II, Encyclical letter, *Evangelium vitae*, March 25, 1995, No 56.

[5] On this issue, see F.G. MORRISEY, "What Makes an Institution Catholic?" in *The Jurist*, 47 (1987), 531-544.

[6] On this issue, see J.H. PROVOST, "The Canonical Aspects of Catholic Identity in the Light of *Ex Corde Ecclesiae*", in *Studia Canonica*, 25 (1991), 155-191.

[7] See Catholic Health Association of the USA, *The Search for Identity: Canonical Sponsorship of Catholic Healthcare*, St. Louis, CHA, 1993, xi-87 p., esp. 59-75 (relating to the future of healthcare and its identity).

Approaching the issue indirectly, we note that four canons tell us that no institution, school, undertaking or association may call itself "catholic" without the authorization of the competent ecclesiastical authorities (see canons 216, 300, 803, §3, and 808). But, beyond that, the Code does not tell us much. Nevertheless, the canons on catholic schools provide us with many elements that can be used.

I believe that, as a result of an analysis of these norms, there are eleven criteria that could be applied to determine catholicity. I will mention these, without placing them in any particular order:

1) The work must operate under the control and direction of a public juridical person (such as a diocese, religious institute, recognized association, etc., see canon 803, §1). This is something like a franchise rule: a person cannot use a trade name without having someone monitor how the "trademark" is being used, so as to protect both the name and the product being marketed. In this case, the trademark name is "catholic".

2) There should be a written document to prove that "catholic" identity has been given (see canon 803, §1). Such a document would spell out conditions, if any, for continued recognition of the catholic status[8].

3) The principles of catholic doctrine must be applied (c. 803, §2); thus, for instance, in a healthcare institution, the approved Code of Ethics would have to be observed[9].

4) Those involved in the work should be noted for their doctrine and uprightness of life (see canon 803, §2). It would be counter-productive for the Church to be engaged in activities where those involved are a counter-sign for what is professed.

5) The work should operate under the authority of the Church (see canon 804, §1). In other words, the diocesan bishop can offer guidance and establish norms and rules to be applied in carrying out apostolic activities in the diocese[10]. Something can be a work of philanthropy or a humanitarian undertaking, but this doesn't necessarily make it apostolic.

[8] For instance, in the USA, listing in the *Official Catholic Directory* implies recognition, with, at times, resulting taxation privileges.

[9] See, for instance, Catholic Health Association of Canada, *Health Care Ethics Guide*, Ottawa, CHAC, 1991, 91 p., approved by the Canadian Conference of Catholic Bishops, February, 1991. In the USA, *Ethical and Religious Directives for Catholic Health Care Services*, Washington, NCCB, 1994, 35 p.

[10] See, for instance, *Health and Health Care. A Pastoral Letter of the American Catholic Bishops*, Washington, USCC, 1981, 14 p.

6) The diocesan bishop would have the right — according to pre-
scribed procedures — to intervene to remove certain persons or to
demand that they be removed (see canon 805). Sometimes, this
right is inscribed in the operative civil documents in relation to
membership on the Board of Directors of an institution or system.

7) There would be a certain right of visitation by the diocesan bishop
(see canon 806), keeping in mind that other canons in the Code out-
line the limitations of a bishop's right to visit persons and works
(see canons 396, 683, 1301, §2, etc.).

8) Even if the work were sponsored by a religious institute, the diocesan bishop would have the right to issue general directives applicable to it (see canon 806, §1).

9) There must be a desire for quality in the work that is at least equal
to that found in similar public institutions (see canon 806, §2).
Indeed, it is of little avail for the Church to operate second-rate
institutions; they become a counter-sign in such cases.

10) The ecclesiastical goods are subject to the norms governing the
administration of temporal goods (see canon 1256).

11) There should be a genuine useful purpose that will foster the well-
being of those being assisted (see canon 114, §3).

b. An "ecclesial" approach

If we remain in this "legal" or, as some would say "legalistic" frame-
work, it is rather easy to state whether a given work or undertaking is
catholic or not. However, the matter is not that simple. For this reason, other
writers prefer the "ecclesial" approach, rather than the "catholic" one.

This approach permits degrees of participation of a juridical entity
within the *communio* of the Church. It belongs to the pastors of the
Church to determine the criteria by which the ecclesial nature of associ-
ations or works may be discerned. The basic principle is to build up the
body of Christ.

c. Criteria derived from different models of the Church

A third approach could also be considered. It arises from principles
operative in models of Church which are not "institutional" in their
thrust, and where there is less direct involvement of church authorities as
such. This approach appears to have been, at least in part, taken by the
Apostolic Constitution, *Ex Corde Ecclesiae*, August 15, 1990, which
recognized many types of Catholic educational institutions, even though

there was no specific link to church authorities[11]. It was further developed by Cardinal Pio Laghi, in August 1995. Speaking of the Catholic identity of universities, he noted:

> One approach held that the Catholic university should be considered as an expression of the very reality of the church itself. ... This position [...] was judged to need a more mature theological reflection.

> The second approach [...] located the Catholic character of the university solely in the fact that the university was inspired by Christian principles. This approach was overwhelmingly rejected as inadequate for distinguishing a Catholic university from any other which chooses to be guided in one way or another by Christian principles.

> A third approach presented itself [...], and this one remains the key to understanding the Catholic identity of the university as embodied in the apostolic constitution. This position holds that the university is Catholic primarily on the basis of its Catholic institutional commitment, involving all who make up the university.

> [... Quoting Pope John Paul II, he continued:] The Catholic identity of your institutions is a complex and vitally important matter. The identity depends upon the explicit profession of Catholicity, on the part of the university as an institution, and also upon the personal conviction and sense of mission on the part of its professors and administrators[12].

Seven possible criteria could be noted were this approach to be adopted:

1) There is a general apostolic purpose — "to help others". This purpose is based on the personal commitment of those involved in the work.
2) The results are appropriate and proportionate to the activity. Thus, they are cost-effective as regards persons, time, and financial resources.
3) The faithful perceive the work as "catholic", that is, as operating under the auspices of a catholic group, etc., and consequently as being trustworthy.
4) There is a form of "catholicity" permeating the establishment, although such is not legislated or contractual (for instance, a general relation to "Rome", catholic traditions, religious signs, the name of the institution, and so forth).

---

[11] See General Norms, Art. 1.3.: "It is contemplated that other Catholic universities, that is, those not established or approved in any of the above ways, ... will conform their existing statutes both to these general norms and to their applications." This article provides for many types of Catholic universities, with various types of bonds linking them to church authorities (see also Art. 2.2).

[12] Cardinal P. LAGHI, "Trust, Cooperation and Dialogue" in *Origins*, 25 (1995-1996), 178.

5) The work is presented as being "christian" without necessarily adding the "catholic" denomination in the title.
6) The work corresponds to a need that is perceived as being in harmony with the purposes of the Church.
7) Government authorities have granted the work certain exemptions that are usually reserved to religious organizations.

d. Criteria based on values to be promoted

The fourth way would entail identifying values that are to be promoted by those responsible for the work. We could list seven of them, noting that they are not incompatible with other criteria listed under the previous approaches.

1) To make certain that we are dealing with a recognized apostolic activity.
2) To be publicly identified with the Catholic Church and guided by its teachings. Responsible stewardship of temporal goods, one of the pillars of the Church's social teachings, requires that we use natural and social resources prudently and in service to all.
3) A preferential option for the poor marks the corporate decisions and calls for particular commitment to those who would otherwise be deprived of quality care.
4) A holistic approach to the human person underlies all activities. Every person is the subject of human dignity, with intrinsic spiritual worth, at every stage of human development.
5) There is respect for the person's needs and right of self-determination. People are inherently social; their dignity is fully realized only in association with others. Our social nature calls for the common good to be served; the self-interest of a few must not compromise the well-being of all.
6) There is respect for human life, for suffering and for death, in the context of a fuller life.
7) We are offering a service, and not simply a commodity exchanged for profit[13].

In all of these approaches, there is one common thread: a link with the diocesan bishop. In fact, we could state that if a work is not in

---

[13] See Cardinal J. BERNARDIN, *Making the Case for Nor-for-Profit Healthcare*, Chicago, January 12, 1995, 16 p.

communion with the diocesan bishop, there is no way that it can be considered catholic (see canon 394, §1). There are many types of schools, colleges and universities that do not meet all the criteria listed above, but which are, nevertheless, in close communion with the bishop. On the other hand, a work could respond to most of the criteria, but if the essential one of communion is missing, then we are not dealing with a catholic undertaking. The bottom line, then, could be presented in the following terms: a work is catholic if the diocesan bishop says it is and is willing to recognize it as such.

II. The Catholic Idenity of Healthcare Institutions[14]

We could take the above-mentioned criteria and apply them literally to our healthcare institutions. Some would easily pass the "catholicity" test, while others might not. However, there is another approach that could be taken in determining the catholic identity of healthcare institutions, and this consists in grouping our data around four critical themes: mission, sponsorship, holistic care, and ethics. These themes, like ingredients in a cake, cannot really be separated one from the other once they have been placed together. Yet, catholicity, like the cake, is more than the sum of the four, although it presupposes them and is based on them.

a. Mission

The mission of the Church is to demonstrate God's love and saving power present in the world. This power, incarnated in the person of Jesus, is clearly seen in the Gospel where we witness Jesus touching, healing, and restoring persons to physical life. The meaning of life becomes expanded to include one's relationship with God and others and hope for life to come.

The mission of Jesus is alive and dynamic. It is not set in one period of time or in a single set of circumstances. Rather, the mission finds unique expression in all times and through a variety of people and institutional structures.

---

[14] Much of this section is taken — even literally — from an undated document issued by the Catholic Health Association of the USA, *A Perspective on How to Approach Catholic Identity in Changing Times. A Working Process Document*, St. Louis, [1994?], 19 p., ms., with bibliography.

The mission of a healthcare organization (such as an institution, a system, an alliance, etc.) drives the entity to actualize its core values and philosophy. It is also a benchmark to evaluate authenticity and effectiveness. Mission should be the driving force by which decisions are made and by which structure and systems are developed.

In this regard, the criteria mentioned in Part I and relating to apostolic purpose and to communion with the diocesan bishop can be applied here.

A catholic healthcare institution should be able to answer clearly and without ambiguity the following question: "What purposes should we serve in today's healthcare environment?" It should also be able to determine the values which shape its corporate culture, using ones that are consistent with the Gospel. These must also become evident both in policies and in practice.

b. *Sponsorship*

Given the changing circumstances affecting healthcare delivery, it is most likely that sponsorship, as we presently know it — operating in the name of and under the authority of a given juridical person — will change its focus from control to influence. There might even come the day when we will no longer be able to influence certain decisions directly. If such occurs, the sponsorship role might even be reduced to one of advocacy: a voice crying in the wilderness.

Traditionally, sponsorship has emphasized a position of corporate strength and independence through ownership and control via reserved powers. Today, as new relations are established with other providers, a presence is required that relies on the ability to influence.

Criteria relating to accountability would be applicable under this heading.

Sponsors must be able to articulate the non-negotiables for the catholic ministry, yet be flexible to choose between total control and having some presence with the power to influence. The process demands a commitment to collaboration with others in order to make the transition to new forms of healthcare delivery.

For this reason, present-day sponsors have to be able to ask themselves what structures or processes will maintain Catholic control or influence. How will they have access to influence? Possibly, through covenants, selection of leadership, board majority, mediation and arbitration processes.

c. Holistic care

Holistic care encompasses the relationship of emotional, intellectual, occupational, physical, and spiritual aspects of personhood through the entire process of healthcare delivery. Simply put, holistic care is sensitivity to the whole person, and not just to a disease or condition that requires medical intervention.

Humans are wonderfully whole in their creation and being. No aspect of the person can ever be considered apart from the totality of personhood. Both in self-assessment and in anticipation of new relationships, it is important to reflect on how the whole, unique person is and will be considered in healthcare ministry.

Criteria relating to quality control would be considered under this heading.

A catholic institution would have to ask itself how it understands holistic care and how this is expressed in the organization's policies, procedures, and practices. Thus, it would have to ask itself also how the spiritual care of persons is integrated into the overall care program. How does this care meet the needs of persons of all denominations?

d. Ethics

Ethics is the discipline that seeks to answer the question: what is good and right for persons as individuals and as members of the human community? Ethics helps us understand how human beings should relate to self, others, and God in order to be fulfilled as human beings.

For Christians, ethical behavior means living our lives in accord with Gospel values, so ethics is never added on to or separate from anything else we do. Continuing analysis and reflection are essential to be certain that who we claim to be is consistent with who we are in practice. Although the catholic tradition is a faith tradition, we believe that catholic teaching is consistent with human reason and insight. Catholic identity demands on-going ethical analysis to ensure that the values at the heart of our catholic tradition are expressed in daily operations at all levels.

Criteria referring to doctrinal issues would fit under this category.

We must recognize that there are many types of ethics that affect the catholicity of an institution or system.

For instance, we have *social ethics* which governs the provision of healthcare services to individual members of the community, thus taking into account the common good. Social ethics seeks to establish among the members of the human community reciprocal relationships. To do this, social ethics reflects specifically upon the rights and responsibilities which the members of the human community have in relationship to the common good which embraces all the material and spiritual goods that are necessary for persons in order that they may live a decent life and fulfill their human destiny.

There are also forms of *corporate ethics* which are expressed in the policies and practices of the institution in regard to social justice. Corporate ethics evaluates the ethical dimension of decisions, policies, and structures which routinely facilitate the management of a healthcare organization's day-to-day operations. The values and disvalues embodied in decisions, policies, and structures affect those persons who have a legitimate interest in the organization. Corporate ethics seeks to promote just relationships among the healthcare organizations and their patients, employees, and the community which they serve.

A third ethical area is what could be called *clinical ethics* whereby respect for the sacredness of life at all stages of development is demonstrated. These ethical issues are concerned with questions that originate in the clinical setting where healthcare is provided. This is a specialized field that includes (but is not limited to) issues related to human genetics and reproduction, treatment decisions at the beginning and end of life, and research involving human subjects.

It is obvious that these four areas cannot be separated. For, one without the other would lead to an incomplete catholic presence. Of course, it is most difficult to evaluate whether these criteria are operative to a required degree, but that does not mean that they can simply be overlooked.

No matter which criteria are used, the institutions or systems have to address a number of new issues that were not in the forefront a decade or two ago. These new questions pose a serious challenge to the future of catholic healthcare, and we shall examine some of them in the third part of this presentation.

III. Contemporary Challenges for Catholic Healthcare

A number of challenges can arise today because of the complex inter-relatedness of the various healthcare providers in a given locality. We can list some of these in turn, again without necessarily following any particular order.

a. Monitoring the observance of ethical directives

Many bishops' conferences have issued ethical and religious directives for the operation of catholic healthcare institutions. While, in theory, all catholic institutions will subscribe to them, we must recognize that the fact of accepting them does not mean that they will always be followed in practice. Indeed, we can ask ourselves how many persons today are truly in a position to know what the catholic position is on a given medical issue. Even priests and religious are sometimes at a loss when faced with new and untested medical procedures. In the future, the Church will need to have even more persons readily available who know the official positions relating to medical ethics and who are able to apply these positions prudently and intelligently.

b. Relationships with the civil legislation

A number of canons in the Code of Canon Law call for the observance of civil legislation, particularly in matters relating to contracts (canon 1290) and the protection of ownership of ecclesiastical goods (canon 1284, §2, 2°).

Difficulties arise when the civil legislation imposes procedures that are against the catholic position. For instance, in some areas, catholic providers — if they are to receive the necessary payments to support the operations — are expected to offer a full range of services, including some that are proscribed by the Church (for instance, abortion, sterilization, withdrawal of nutrition, and so forth). While in some areas there are clauses respecting the conscience of individuals who do not wish to become directly involved in proscribed services, these exceptions have not always been recognized as belonging to the institution itself.

c. Alienation of church property[15]

The norms relating to the alienation of church property have been carefully observed in many jurisdictions. However, given the fact today

[15] On this issue, see F.G. MORRISEY, "The Alienation of Temporal Goods in Contemporary Society", in *Studia Canonica*, 29 (1995), 293-316.

that buildings are becoming liabilities rather than assets, it seems incongruous to place so much emphasis on the bricks and mortar, and not on the work itself.

This becomes even more acute where a system of "capitation" is in effect, that is, where persons are part of an insurance programme. The institution that is related to the insurance plan receives a given amount per annum for each subscriber. If the subscriber does not use the services, then the institution makes money. However, the more the institution is used, the less profit it makes. While in previous times, a hospital was considered to be very profitable if it had a high occupancy rate, today this becomes a liability. What, then, in such circumstances, remains to be alienated? Canonists have not yet found a satisfactory answer to this question.

d. Dealing with "for profit" providers

While the Catholic Church has consistently considered that its basic services are dispensed not on a fee for service basis, but rather on a charitable basis, today many for profit providers are seeking to take over and operate catholic institutions, while respecting their catholicity.

For some persons, this is a total contradiction[16]. For others, this can be tolerated. The jury is still out on this point. Perhaps it might be possible to consider certain types of joint ventures, but, if the profit factor becomes predominant, it can be asked to what point personal and corporate ethics will prevail[17].

e. Cooperation with other providers[18]

While, in theory, it is easy enough to consider the possibility of entering into joint ventures with other catholic providers, this is not always easy, particularly when the catholic institution is the only one in the geographical district[19]. To what extent can catholic institutions cooperate actively and directly with other institutions, for instance, with those that provide abortions, even though they would not perform abortions themselves?

[16] On this issue, see J. CURLEY, "For-Profit Chains Seeking to Buy Catholic Hospitals", in *Origins*, 25 (1995-1996), 78-79.

[17] See *Origins*, 25 (1995-1996), 79, marginal note.

[18] On this issue, see F.G. MORRISEY, "Canonical Issues to Anticipate and Resolve in Mergers and Joint Ventures involving Catholic Health-care Institutions" in F.R. AZNAR GIL, ed., *Magister canonistarum*, Salamanca, Universidad Pontificia, 1994, 215-236.

[19] See Archdiocese of Chicago, *Protocol for Evaluating Joint Ventures and Affiliations Relating to Catholic Health Care Ministry*, Chicago, August 31, 1994, and the accompanying remarks of Cardinal J. BERNARDIN, 11 p.

Some people have adopted a "carving out" policy, stating that a given section or portion of a hospital or clinic is not subject to catholic directives, even though the system itself is. For others, a "carving in" approach is used: the entire system remains non-catholic, but the catholic component, which can be a small part of the whole, observes the catholic teaching and practice. In all such instances, there is a potential risk for scandal, which must be prudently evaluated, taking other factors into account.

For instance, and this is most delicate, we can say that in general Catholics respect and observe the Church's teaching relating to abortion. Therefore, to enter into a partnership with an institution that is known officially as an abortion clinic would cause serious scandal. However, when it comes to matters relating to sterilization and reproductive technologies, there is not the same "approval rate" among Catholics. Thus, the risk of scandal in a given geographical area could be much less in the case of cooperation with an institution that provides such services. This, of course, does not necessarily justify greater cooperation, but it certainly complicates the issue. The diocesan bishop is the judge in such instances, and very often he is faced with a terrible dilemma.

f. Dealing with insurance providers

Since today in some parts of the world it is the insurance providers who determine which doctor shall treat the person and which hospital a prospective patient will frequent, and since many providers insist that a full range of services be offered if the hospital or institution wishes to be part of the payment plan, hospitals are faced with the dilemma of choosing between being willing to offer certain proscribed services, or else see their doors close for lack of proper and adequate financing.

The moral norms of direct and indirect cooperation come into play here. It is for this reason that many healthcare providers have sought to establish links with other institutions that provide the services that insurance companies insist must be offered.

Without any doubt, this can lead — and quite quickly — to a watering down of catholic principles and practice. There comes a point — and I don't know where it is — where, for all practical purposes, the institution no longer meets the criteria for being a catholic hospital because the ethical and religious directives are only partially observed. The challenge is one that is being faced in many ways.

g. Establishing networks

For some strange reason, it is a fact that Catholics often find it very difficult to cooperate with other Catholics. They would sooner deal with another institution that has no direct or religious affiliation.

If catholic providers enter into networks with secular or other religious, but non-catholic, providers, it doesn't take too long before the catholic institution is swallowed up by the larger group.

For this reason, a number of bishops have issued protocols relating to the approval to be given to joint ventures with other providers. Rightly so, they want catholic institutions to cooperate with other catholic institutions.

Today, as sponsoring religious institutes are facing a diminishing number of qualified members to assure the operation of their institutions, there is more openness than in the past to foster inter-congregational cooperation. However, this is not always easy. We simply have to consider the outroar when a bishop decides to close a small parish and merge it with another one! Yet, there are so many instances when religious institutes are working together and even pooling their financial resources to ensure the viability of their ministries.

Personally, I find it very difficult to deal with the phenomenon of non-cooperation. If Catholics are unable to cooperate with other Catholics, then we can ask ourselves what type of witness are we giving to society. In fact, if we refuse to cooperate with one another, it might be stated that we deserve to disappear because we are offering a counter-testimony, rather than a witness to the unity of the Church and its mission.

h. The factors driving our apostolic endeavours

It can be asked today whether the Church's healthcare operations are truly mission-driven, or whether it is finance that is the driving force.

We all realize that appropriate financial arrangements are necessary if we are to offer quality care, care that is at least as outstanding as that offered by secular institutions (see canon 806), but, when the primary concern becomes the financial "bottom line", we can ask to what extent we are continuing to offer quality charity care to the indigent and to those in need.

This is one more challenge to be faced by administrators today.

i. The change to out-patient services

With the on-going developments in medical science, many interventions that previously would have required several days of hospitalization, today can be performed on an out-patient basis. For instance, with the use of lasers, cataract operations can now be performed in a few minutes and the patient is sent home within an hour or two of the operation.

It is obvious that, in such circumstances, there is little opportunity for an institution to exert its "catholic" influence on someone who is within its walls for only a couple of hours.

It might be, then, that our focus will have to shift from acute care to extended care and care for the elderly where a holistic approach can be better put into effect.

Of course, with extended care, there arises today the issue of euthanasia and the responsible use of limited temporal resources. Just as the Church had to face the abortion issue over the past decade, so too it will now have to address the so-called "death with dignity" and "assisted suicide" issues.

Likewise, we will have to watch the use of vocabulary. People now speak of "abortion rights" and "reproductive rights" and a person's "rights over his or her body", when no such natural rights exist, at least in an absolute sense. Likewise, they are now beginning to speak of the "right to die". Again, such a right is not an absolute. It will be important to make certain that we don't get caught up in a debate based on faulty vocabulary that could color the issue in such a way that there is no healthy exit from it.

Conclusion

It is obvious to any of us today that the Church has numerous challenges to face if it is to continue to offer to the world the health-giving image of Jesus Christ. Perhaps the time has come for us to divest ourselves of some of the large institutions that give little witness to the charity of Christ which urges us on.

When we see that the financial reports of some catholic healthcare providers are issued not in thousands or even millions of dollars, but rather in billions, we realize that we have come a long way from the early days.

Personally, I am spending much of my time these months with catholic healthcare institutions, trying to find ways whereby we can continue our presence in the ministry, without compromising our values. There are geographical "solutions" which can be applied in one part of the world, but not in another. There are times when some of our institutions no longer answer a real need of society; they probably should be closed. There are other institutions whose quality leaves something to be desired. They too should be looked at and either beefed up or closed.

The Church's heritage is one that it is not ready to give up. It must find new ways of exercising it in a changed, secularized society. The answer does not lie in retreating from the battlefield, but rather in making certain that we are operating on principles that are sure and are in conformity with the Church's moral and ethical teachings.

The challenge is great and each of us, in one way or another, will be called upon to do our part to help overcome the obstacles.

Prof. dr. Francis G. Morrisey
Saint Paul University,
Ottawa, Canada.